A collection of voices to unite, inspire, and create brighter pathways for women in security.

VOCAL LANTERNS

EDITED BY
**ARIAN AVILA &
JENNIFER WALTERS**

FOREWORD BY
LAUREN BEAN BUITTA
FOUNDER & CEO, GIRL SECURITY

ARIAN AVILA AND JENNIFER WALTERS

Vocal Lanterns

A collection of voices to unite, inspire, and create brighter pathways for women in security.

First published by A-Dub Productions LLC 2025

Copyright © 2025 by Arian Avila and Jennifer Walters

All rights reserved. No part of this publication may be reproduced, stored or transmitted in any form or by any means, electronic, mechanical, photocopying, recording, scanning, or otherwise without written permission from the publisher. It is illegal to copy this book, post it to a website, or distribute it by any other means without permission.

Designations used by companies to distinguish their products are often claimed as trademarks. All brand names and product names used in this book and on its cover are trade names, service marks, trademarks and registered trademarks of their respective owners. The publishers and the book are not associated with any product or vendor mentioned in this book. None of the companies referenced within the book have endorsed the book.

First edition

ISBN: 979-8-9930676-0-5

Cover art by Nick Young
Editing by Nanette Levin

This book was professionally typeset on Reedsy.
Find out more at reedsy.com

For Anya, Miles, Koa, and Olivia

Continue to carry forth the torch of love, hope, and strength that has burned within your souls since your first breath. We love you.

Remember, no matter where we are, who we work for, or what we do each day:

Speak your truth.
Be Brave.
Be bold and beautiful.
Embrace your flaws, celebrate your wins.
Hold your ground, spread love and take no shit.
Don't play the victim, become the warrior.
Know your worth, protect your energy and tell your story.
Share your magic, laugh loud and proud and don't sweat the small stuff.
Blow your own damn mind.

Brittany Galli
Founder, Global Women in Security Alliance

Contents

Foreword ii
Preface vi
Introduction 1

I Forging Unconventional Paths

1 Lighting the Way 5
2 Navigating Entry and Career Advancement 28

II Thriving in the Field

3 Finding Your Voice, Building Your Brand, and Dealing with... 51
4 Men Can Be Powerful Supporters 74
5 The Power of Mentorship and Sisterhood 83
6 The Security Life Balance 91

III Taking It to the Next Level

7 Security Entrepreneurship 111
8 Shaping the Future of Security 122

9 Conclusion 128
Recommended Resources for Continued Growth & Connection 130
Acknowledgments 131
Contributor Bios 133
About the Editors 159

Foreword

I often say that I am the moral of the story of Girl Security, an organization I formally founded in 2019 to explore both how girls and women perceive national security as a career sector and to consider the most effective model for advancing diverse populations of youth into the security sector.

Like many of the professionals you will encounter in this book, my path into security was nonlinear. As a teen, I was especially interested in understanding regional conflict, gender inequality, and geopolitics. This became a line through in my career, until I landed at my first job post-college working as a national security policy analyst with a Chicago-based think tank shortly after the terrorist attacks of September 11, 2001.

I had never experienced an environment like national security. On one hand, it embodied the kind of work I sought—purpose, service, and being part of something bigger than myself. On the other hand, I had rarely seen so few women in a space, except in construction, where I worked during college and was often the only woman. And, of the women I did meet and have the privilege to observe, I was always particularly impressed by their ability to thread the needle on highly complex security issues. I wanted to see more women and to see their ideas represented.

Like too many women, I experienced workplace violence early into my career, which led me to another path that was transformative, working on affordable housing and civil rights in my hometown of Chicago. That decade shaped my understanding of security in ways I could never have learned otherwise; without it, my view of the broader security ecosystem would be painfully narrow. Inequality is compounded for women of color, the LGBTQ+ communities, persons with disabilities, and many other diverse groups that are too often marginalized. This is a deficit for our national resilience, our collective security, and our democracy.

The confluence of these experiences provided a foundation for Girl Security, and in over the past six years, I have encountered countless incredible security leaders who inspire me every day to invest my whole self into ensuring Girl Security can fulfill its mission and theory of change, to forge a new paradigm for security that values the perspectives, skills, and contributions of every single individual who seeks this path.

There are always those who carry the light during dark times, not because they seek recognition for the light they carry, but because they were called to some purpose that imbued them with spark that they humbly nurtured. The stories within these pages illuminate a fundamental truth that has driven so many of us, which is a call to simply help others. And, as you will read, there is no single path to purpose in security. What these remarkable practitioners share is not a common starting point, but a common commitment: to making the world more secure through their unique and selfless contributions.

As I often say, "A nation is only as secure as its populations," and when vast populations remain excluded from security careers, we create fundamental vulnerabilities in how we think about and approach security itself. It is a flaw that is only exacerbated when limited viewpoints are involved. The origin stories you will encounter here prove that strength lies not in uniformity, but in the rich diversity of experiences, perspectives, and paths that lead talented individuals to this critical field.

From Jennifer Walters, who discovered her calling not through traditional law enforcement channels but through a chance encounter with a database administrator role that opened her eyes to the excitement of protection work, to Pranoti Surve, who pivoted from investigative journalism to become an intelligence analyst during the 2008 financial crisis, each story reveals how seemingly unrelated experiences can become the foundation for a security career. These leaders didn't just "fall into" security; they brought with them the accumulated wisdom of their journeys, creating value precisely because of their diverse backgrounds, not in spite of them.

What strikes me most profoundly about these narratives is how they challenge the narrow definitions that have historically constrained our industry.

Mary Gates discovered her passion for corporate security through a temporary assignment that revealed the complexity and importance of a field she had never considered. Jessica Hern's path from international affairs to intelligence analysis shows how global perspectives enhance security thinking. Melody Wen's deeply personal connection to 9/11 as a New York City resident whose mother worked at the Twin Towers transformed tragedy into a lifelong commitment to resilience.

These are not stories of people adapting themselves to fit predetermined molds. These are stories of people reshaping the very landscape of security through their authentic selves, their unique insights, and their refusal to accept that there is only one way to contribute to this vital work.

The metaphor of lighting the way resonates deeply with Girl Security's mission. Since 2019, we have worked to expand national security for thousands of youth by recognizing that the national security sector is far more expansive and includes the entire federal government, state and local government, the private sector, academia, STEM, civil society, and more. Every girl and young person who learns about cybersecurity or who discovers threat analysis and every person from an underrepresented community who finds their place in this field becomes a lantern, illuminating possibilities for others who might never have seen themselves in this work and contributing to a collective purpose.

The contributors whose stories grace these pages understand something fundamental: representation matters as a strategic imperative. When Lillian Teng writes about how women professors shaped her trajectory into cybersecurity, she highlights the power of seeing oneself reflected in roles of expertise, authority, and influence. When Arian Avila describes how childhood fascination with Inspector Gadget and Carmen Sandiego translated into a passion for crime analysis, she reveals how inspiration can emerge from the most unexpected places, if one is open to seeing the connections.

What gives me tremendous hope is how these stories demonstrate that the pipeline into security careers is not broken, but too narrow. Every woman who found her way here through "happy accidents," personal tragedy, intellectual curiosity, or sheer determination has widened that pipeline for those who follow. They are living proof that security needs economists and journalists, psychologists and international relations experts, teachers and technologists, mothers and daughters who bring their full selves to the work of protection.

The courage required to share these origin stories should not be underestimated. In revealing their moments of uncertainty, their non-traditional paths, their struggles to prove themselves in rooms full of skeptics, these women offer something invaluable: belonging. Future generations must see their own unconventional journeys as assets to leverage and then to create a sense of belonging for those who follow.

As you read these stories, I invite you to consider not just how these women found security, but how security found them and was transformed in the process. Notice how their diverse backgrounds didn't dilute their effectiveness but enhanced it. Observe how their "outsider" perspectives often led to innovative solutions. Recognize how their willingness to question assumptions and challenge traditional approaches made the entire field stronger.

The lanterns these women carry light more than just their own paths forward. They illuminate the vast, untapped potential that exists when we expand our understanding of who belongs in security and how they might arrive. They show us that the future of security lies not in replicating the past, but in embracing the complexity of human experience and translating it into more robust, more inclusive, more effective protection for all.

In the end, these origin stories are not about the past, but about possibility. They are about the girls and young women who will read these pages and see themselves not as outsiders looking in, but as future leaders already carrying within them everything they need to light their own way forward.

The path to security has always been illuminated by those brave enough to carry the flame. These women have lit the way for countless others to follow. As we say at Girl Security, together, we are building the future of security - by design, not default.

Lauren Bean Buitta
Founder and CEO, Girl Security

Preface

This book was created for you and for the future yous who will follow. Our industry only thrives when we lift one another up. That's why all proceeds from this book support **Girl Security**, a nonprofit preparing the next generation of women in security through mentorship, training, and career opportunities. We invite you to learn more and get involved in this vital work, helping to shape the future of women in security, by visiting www.girlsecurity.org.

Introduction

Lanterns have always been more than just a source of light. They are symbols of guidance, of hope, of resilience. They show us the way forward when the path is unclear, and they remind us that even in the darkest spaces, we are never entirely alone.

When I (Arian) stepped into corporate security for the first time, I didn't know what to expect or who I'd find. Jennifer Walters was one of the very first teammates I met. I was lucky enough to share more than a cubicle wall with her. From the start, we were each other's support system, and over time, **we became each other's lanterns**. That creative energy between us is what made this book come to life.

Within these pages, you'll find the warm glow of *vocal lanterns*. These are real stories from professionals across the security industry who have not only found their way but are also lighting the way for others. You'll hear from women protecting CEOs and global organizations, cybersecurity experts thwarting digital threats, security strategists safeguarding corporate assets, and entrepreneurs building cutting-edge security startups from the ground up. You'll also hear from allies who have taken that torch to help light the path for others. Their voices reflect true inclusion, advocacy, and what we need more of to further the presence of women in security.

* * *

A note on structure. This isn't your typical leadership or industry guide. Rather than pages filled with analysis or commentary, what you'll find here are raw, insightful, and deeply personal experiences presented in the contributors' own words. We asked the questions; they provided honest, thought-provoking, and practical answers. Our Q&A style format is intentional, allowing you to gain insight into lived experiences through beautiful, authentic reflections. You can read straight through or skip around. There is no single path, like there's no single right path into security. These stories are here to connect with you:

- The surprising ways women drove toward – or stumbled into – the industry and the myriad paths available to get here.
- Practical advice for developing your network and advancing your career.
- Ideas for building your brand, owning your dopeness, and balancing humility with self-promotion to increase your visibility.
- Perspectives on navigating bias, stereotypes, and microaggressions while staying true to yourself.
- The power of mentorship and sisterhood, and how we lift as we climb... because none of us get through this journey alone.
- A look at allies and how true change requires partnership, including how influence is used to open doors and challenge the status quo.
- Honest reflections on security-life integration, setting boundaries in a 24/7 industry, managing guilt, and making space for self-care.
- Stories of entrepreneurship, for those ready to build something of their own and redefine what leadership looks like in security.
- And finally, a vision for shaping the future of security, together. A future where inclusion isn't an afterthought but a foundation.

Our hope is that as you read these stories, you'll see pieces of your journey reflected here or glimpses of the path you might still be carving. We hope you feel seen, encouraged, and challenged to take up space, share your voice, and help light the way for others.

The more we share our experiences, our lessons, and our light, the brighter the way becomes for all of us.

I

Forging Unconventional Paths

1

Lighting the Way

Before we can light the path for others, we have to start with our own stories. And for many of us, those stories began in the dark.

We asked a simple question: **What's your security origin story?**

The answers were anything but simple, and they led to so many meaningful, unexpected journeys. Some women stumbled into this field by chance. They'll tell you they "fell into it" without even realizing where they were headed at first. Others chased it down with purpose, driven by a desire to make things better, or a curiosity to understand how the world works and how it sometimes falls apart. And some never pictured themselves here at all, until a door cracked open, or they decided to open one themselves.

The stories in this chapter come from women across all corners of the security world and remind us why we belong here. Their experiences are different; their backgrounds are different (and that's exactly the point!). There is no single 'right' way to find your place in this field. But by sharing how we started, we help illuminate the possibilities for those still searching for their way.

These are our beginnings. The moments that brought us here.

Finding Security Through Serendipity

"Sometimes you find your path, sometimes it finds you." - Max Brooks

"I worked for a prominent Louisiana bank, rotating between locations and departments, where I learned various duties and could perform just about any job across the organization. One day, I received a call to work in the Corporate Security Department. I immediately told my supervisor, "I have no idea how to be a guard."

> **Looking back, I was part of the naivete surrounding the importance of a Corporate Security Team and all they do, every day, without recognition or applause.**

I worked with the Security Director on a complex employee investigation. It was fascinating work, challenging me in new ways, causing me to think differently, and tapping into various parts of my personality and creativity. Growing up, I always felt a deep desire to take on responsibility and protect those around me. Whether it was standing up for a friend or protecting the strays in the neighborhood, the instinct to safeguard others came naturally. This innate desire exploded once I began my brief stint in the Security Department nearly forty years ago. As I concluded my assignment, I told the Security Director, "Please think of me if you ever have an opening on your team." Thankfully, I did not wait long before the Security Director called and offered me a role. I would be starting at an entry-level position, but I did not care. I had an opportunity to gain experience, develop, and explore a career in a field that aligned with my values, challenged me, and allowed me to make a tangible difference! I was drawn to the idea of being a part of a solution, actively deterring risks, and responding effectively when challenges arise."

- Mary Gates

"**I never intended to work in security**. My passion was international affairs and learning about other cultures, but a career path in that field wasn't clear to me during college. After college, I found a job at the U.S. Department of Justice supporting international rule of law development. I organized trainings for prosecutors and judges in Asia, which allowed me to travel extensively. I happened to be in this role on 9/11. My office was one block from the White House, which was the intended destination of the fourth plane that went down in Pennsylvania. I also had just completed a training in the Philippines on countering terrorist financing. Suddenly, I was being asked to replicate this training in fifty countries and become an expert on jihadist terrorism. I was brought into classified intelligence briefings and represented the Department of Justice in cross-agency meetings. I wanted to go back to school, so I decided to move to New York and attend Columbia University's School of International and Public Affairs. My experiences working in the counter-terrorism area pushed me toward an International Security Policy concentration, where I was introduced to intelligence and military policy. My summer internship in between my two years in graduate school was in the intelligence area, and I obtained a higher security clearance. I decided that working in intelligence was the best way for me to further my passion for international affairs, and I found a job as an intelligence analyst. I loved it. I knew more than anyone about my area of responsibility and was using my knowledge and interest in international affairs every day. But I was far from my midwestern home and wanted a life that was out of reach in the expensive D.C. area. A family emergency pushed me to start looking for a job in the private sector. It was challenging to translate my intelligence analyst skills into job applications in the private sector because people often struggled to understand my resume. I was lucky to find a boss on a corporate security team who also came from the intelligence community and saw potential in me. I started working on travel security, incident and crisis management, and building out a basic intelligence capability, mostly focused on risk to business. The scope of my work in the security field has changed over time as I developed business acumen and grew into enterprise risk management and business resilience."

- Jessica Hern

"In 1996, I left college temporarily to participate in a work abroad exchange, where I was supposed to spend three months working in the UK before returning to finish my degree. That trip would turn into a three-year-long trip around the world where I lived and worked in the UK, Ireland, and Australia, and traveled through Asia, Oceania and Europe – mesmerized by the world that was out there and all of the things I was learning by being out in it. One of those things was spending several months in Thailand and Malaysia during the Asian financial crisis in 1997-1998, which is where **I started to understand the tangible reality of global economics and its macro and micro impacts on security**. When I finally returned to school it was in an International Studies Program, where I received a National Security Education Scholarship that sent me back to Asia – this time to Vietnam – and eventually resulted in my landing a job with the US Defense Intelligence Agency – which again led me back overseas – this time in a work capacity. I eventually made my way to the private sector and was one of the early private sector intelligence hires in oil and gas in 2007."

- Meredith Wilson

> **My journey supports the notion that you don't have to have a traditional security background to be successful in the security industry.**
> I landed in security by transitioning from an international trade compliance role, where I had deep knowledge of a corporation's supply chain, and then moved into supply chain security. That move started my pathway to security program development and deployment, which has been a foundational skill of my success. My career has followed a path of developing programs from nothing to evolving existing programs to their next maturity level.
>
> *- Kirsten Provence*

"**I had been an HR professional for nearly thirty years and came into security accidentally**. While handling an employee separation questionably (think meeting a firearms instructor in the equivalent of a dark alley to collect their gun safe and other belongings after hours), I was encouraged by my security partners to learn more about behavioral threat assessment and management (BTAM) and attended my first Association of Threat Assessment Professionals[1] (ATAP) meeting. Multidisciplinary threat teams made so much sense to me, and I was all in from that first meeting.

I began coordinating training sessions for our Northwest ATAP Chapter, led the chapter as president, and have been involved at the national level for many years – I have unofficially given myself the title of World Expert at Threat Conference Scavenger Hunts. Along the way, I began sharing thoughts and practical suggestions for bridging the gap between Security and HR, partnered with Dr. Nathan Brooks on *How Not to Hire a Psychopath*[2], and expanded my security interests into HR and Insider Threat, plus became involved with ASIS[3] and the Human Threat Management Steering Committee. And yet, I described myself as "security-adjacent" and not actually part of security itself. An ambassador of sorts between two disciplines filled with historical tension. Then, this past year brought two moments of change. First, a brilliant security expert who brings a behavioral health perspective to workplace violence prevention referred to me as a mentor.

I was profoundly struck by the realization that, while I have questioned my role within this community, others see me differently—a powerful reminder of the value of role models and the need to move beyond perceived inadequacies.

---

[1] Association of Threat Assessment Professionals (ATAP), founded in 1992 as a nonprofit organization representing law enforcement, mental health, corporate security, and other professionals, provides a forum for education, training, and collaboration around stalking, threats, and homeland security issues. Check out atapworldwide.org for more info.

[2] Melissa Muir, "How Not to Hire a Psychopath," *How Not to Hire a Psychopath*, accessed August 22, 2025, https://www.hownottohireapsychopath.com/melissa-muir.

[3] ASIS International, the leading professional organization for security management professionals worldwide, provides certification, standards, and global networking opportunities for practitioners. See asisonline.org for more info.

In the words of Marianne Williamson, "Our deepest fear is not that we are inadequate. Our deepest fear is that we are powerful beyond measure." Second, I led a training in threat assessment and management. Not the HR aspect of it, not the partnership between two disciplines, the core content that I've studied for fifteen years. I realized when I was introduced that the audience thought of me as an expert, and that I've thought deeply about this work for many years. And it took me until I wasn't self-identifying as a security neighbor and instead as an expert in an aspect of security, that I fully embraced the security community that has long welcomed me."

- Melissa Muir

"**Growing up, I wanted to be a sports journalist and newscaster** like my father. He convinced me that I wouldn't be successful. So, I decided I was going to be a lawyer, but law schools chose to ignore my GPA and focus on my low LSAT scores, so no law school. Since I liked law, I shifted to criminal justice, and it was here that I found my place to serve, to be a team player, and to change perspectives."

- Wendy Bashnan

"Two critical decisions shaped my career path. First, I pursued a dual Master's in Business and Leadership at a women's liberal arts college, and second, I actively engaged and committed to being part of several women-in-business organizations. Both were pivotal investments in myself that significantly accelerated my career trajectory and built connections that led me to the many chapters of my life thus far. My first introduction to the security industry came as a management consultant with a boutique, woman-owned firm in the San Francisco Bay Area. Assigned to a large healthcare security project, I was thrown headfirst into the world of cameras, network video recorders, and access control systems. To my surprise, I was captivated. It was clear the industry was evolving, and opportunities were expanding. From there, I focused my consulting efforts on risk, cybersecurity, and corporate security. Through this work, I developed a deep understanding of the business of security, particularly what it takes to lead an organization through transformational change, and was subsequently tapped to join a security organization as Vice President of Security Strategy."

- Liz Rice

"I didn't want a career in security when I was a kid. In fact, I didn't know that if you smushed the three words *career in security* together, they meant something.

> **I thought *security* was the dude at the mall in a uniform that chased shoplifters as a part-time job to get him through college**. I thought *security* was the sleepy old man at the front desk of my mom's office building. I didn't want to do those things.

What I did want to do was write. I started writing in middle school, mainly goofy stuff to entertain my friends when we were bored. This translated into an excitement that my classmates thought was weird whenever we were assigned a research essay. I had lots of opinions, and I loved crafting together magical strings of words that I was confident would convince even the most skeptical that my thoughts were the right thoughts. I didn't care about grades. I cared about shifting perspectives through my idealistic (although often naive) views on how to change the world to make it a safer place for all to live peacefully, for all to thrive.

I suspect that this desire to make this world a better place stemmed from a childhood full of uncertainty and chaos. I grew up in Pontiac, Michigan, where winters were cold, particularly when the power was shut off because the bills were not reliably paid. I experienced homelessness for the first time at age eight and learned early on that fending for myself and not expecting anyone to take care of me was a hard truth of life. **I wanted nothing more than to feel normal and safe and figure out how I could help make others feel the same**. I wasn't physically strong, nor did I consider myself particularly brave, but I knew that my pen could form the words I felt my voice could not, and decided my path to making an impact would be through a career in journalism.

I took a trip to visit family in Charlotte, North Carolina. It was warm, bright, shiny, new - all the things that I wasn't used to seeing where I lived. I decided it was worth looking at job opportunities because if I found something, I wasn't going to go back. The stars aligned and landed me in a job at the local newspaper. I wasn't writing, but it seemed to be a step in the right direction. I enrolled in school in Charlotte and felt like I was on my way to making my dreams come true, but reality tapped me on the shoulder and told me maybe not.

A year in, I realized that I hated working at the newspaper. After spending some time with the writers, I learned that their day-to-day work wasn't for me, so I applied and was hired for a random security database administrator job. From my first day, I was in love. These folks were doing all kinds of cool stuff – talking to bank tellers who had just been robbed, sending the police to catch the bad guys, and in my section of the room, keeping the systems and equipment that enabled that work running. My excitement turned to ideas that I bombarded my boss with until I eventually wore him down, and he gave me an opportunity to prove myself."

- Jennifer Walters

"After my international studies in college right as the wall was coming down in Berlin, I worked at UNICEF headquarters in New York City. At UNICEF, there was more gender equality than I experienced in corporate life. There were men and women in leadership roles. While this was a dream job in many ways, and it was invigorating to be there, learning about my region and contributing to reviewing an actual publication, it was an entry-level position. I realized that I should go to graduate school. I managed to obtain a grant to study abroad, in Madrid. I received a master's degree in International Cooperation and Development, thinking I would go back to humanitarian work. It turned out life had other plans.

Before LinkedIn, video calls, cell phones and even texting, one would meet with a headhunter, in person, armed with paper resumes as part of a job search. This is exactly what I did in my hometown of Miami. I was intrigued when she [the headhunter] mentioned an opportunity as a "threat analyst" with a large company, and after an interview with a dynamic, charismatic, interesting person who ended up being one of the best mentors I have ever had, I accepted a job with Exxon (pre ExxonMobil) as a regional threat analyst. With my idealistic mindset, I figured I would stay at this position for six months, save money, and then return to my mission to 'save the world.' Ten years later, I was still working with ExxonMobil, having traveled the world, met amazing people, most of which I am still in touch with today, and learned the basics about how to overlay geopolitical curiosity with business interests in a way I never imagined existed."

- Eva Deren

"I never thought I'd end up in the security industry. **As a kid growing up in San Diego, my dream was to become a SeaWorld trainer and work with Shamu!**[4] Decades later, and without ever swimming with orcas, I realize I've swum through and against currents I couldn't have imagined. Admittedly, some of those currents didn't necessarily feel meaningful at the time; in fact, there were roles that felt downright unhelpful. However, those steps that seemed like detours turned out to be the most pivotal experiences of my career. I approached each opportunity even if it didn't align with what I thought was my path upward with curiosity and humility. Those opportunities introduced me to people I wouldn't have otherwise collaborated with, including some who were overtly reluctant toward a newcomer in their field. But by approaching each individual with a genuine interest in learning about their path, the initial reluctance faded. And as I listened, I shared my own journey, revealing that even though this particular step perhaps wasn't planned, I was humbled to be part of it and eager to learn. I showed up with that curiosity and humility each time, and I experienced how that combination disarmed even the most reluctant of partners. This provided me comfort: the times I felt I didn't have the book smarts or the field experience, I always had my willingness and humility, no matter my previous role or what I studied. And, the gifts of

---

[4] Shamu was the name given to the first female orca at SeaWorld in 1965 and later became the stage name for the park's killer whale shows, serving as both a brand identity and cultural icon.

these experiences continue to deliver: **If I had stayed on the path I planned for myself as a child, I may never have gotten to swim outside the tank. I don't know what it feels like to swim with killer whales, but I do know how fulfilling it is to connect with another human, learn, and keep swimming."**

– Michelle La Plante

Moments and Events That Inspired Purpose

"The wound is the place where the light enters you." – Rumi

"My security origin story is crystal clear. It was 2004. I was conducting research and teaching in Germany on a Fulbright Fellowship when the Madrid train bombings occurred, killing nearly 200 people and injuring more than 2,000. Unlike in the U.S., **German news outlets showed uncensored images, and they shook me.** Less than three years after 9/11, I knew in that moment that terrorism was one of the defining security threats of our time. That fall, I entered graduate school to pursue a master's in International Politics, focusing on international security."

– Jessica Martinez

"A childhood trip to the Middle East had an immense impact on me. Learning about the region and its history led me to go back years later for a year in university, enrolling in a Conflict and Rapprochement program. Living in Jerusalem, I met influential Israeli and Palestinian scholars and politicians, but also saw a lot of volatility in a year when the Prime Minister was assassinated and there was a campaign of bus bombings. I learned so much traveling through Egypt, Jordan, Turkey, the West Bank, and around Israel, from people who had such a long history of conflict.

> **Experiencing how they handled it personally and as nations assured me that I wanted to work in the foreign relations or security field in some capacity.**

So I moved to Washington, DC after graduating. After lucking into meeting a few amazing women already in the field, I got a job with the State Department's Overseas Security Advisory Council. And that is where it all began!"

— *Mary Hackman*

"My origin story was sparked by the events of September 11, 2001. Growing up in New York City and as the child of Chinese immigrant parents, I spent most weekends in Chinatown. While the world watched the events unfold on television or heard them on the radio, I witnessed firsthand how 9/11 impacted the city, especially Lower Manhattan, both immediately after and in the years that followed. Since I was a child, my mom worked at the Twin Towers, and fortunately, she was off work that day. I vividly remember her journey in navigating the emotional and psychological aftermath; I also remember how the world came together for our city and how much more resilient we became. While my path to security started with a uniquely personal and deeply sad experience, it profoundly shaped my perspective. **My love for the city, my community, and my family are the driving forces behind my commitment to making the world more resilient and safer.**"

— *Melody Wen*

"Growing up, a clear expectation was the importance of giving back. I volunteered in a hospital as a Candy Striper. One afternoon, when I was helping in the ER, several first responders came in with a clear purpose; they had a young boy on a stretcher with his hand in the air. His hand was wrapped, but I could tell he was bleeding badly. I learned later that his father had put the boy's hand into a garbage disposal. I was shocked and horrified. It was a life-changing moment for me. It shattered my assumption that parents always protected their children. It was inconceivable to me that some parents hurt their children. **It sparked a lifelong commitment to seek justice and protect the vulnerable.** Initially, I planned to pursue law school and become a judge. As a criminal justice major, I was drawn to the idea of holding people accountable. In college, through coursework led by attorneys, I came to understand that the law exists largely in shades of gray—not the black-and-white thinking I once held. This prompted me to shift focus toward law enforcement, where I could be more action-oriented and directly involved in investigations. After graduation, I applied widely while I was working as a probation and parole officer. At the time of my graduation, to become a police officer, I would have had to fund my own entrance into the academy, which was something I couldn't afford. I turned to federal law enforcement and ultimately found my home with the Naval Criminal Investigative Service (NCIS).

Serving as an NCIS special agent for twenty-five years took me to eight different duty stations around the world and allowed me to specialize in violent crime. Through my work, I became interested in preventing crimes instead of only responding to them, and learned about behavioral threat assessment. It changed my future. I saw a need for this work and brought the idea back to my agency to develop NCIS' Threat Management Unit."

- Dorian Van Horn

"I wasn't originally looking for a career in intelligence or security. I wasn't sure what I wanted to do after my undergraduate studies, so I took a gap year studying Mandarin in Beijing and traveling in Asia. One of my American classmates had a relative who worked for the Central Intelligence Agency (CIA) and they encouraged me to apply for a graduate program sponsored by the CIA and to consider a career in the US government intelligence community. It was an interesting time for me when I was abroad - I had never fully realized how lucky I was that my parents had left Asia for America in the 60's until I spent that time in China. My family had so much more opportunity because of my parents' decision and I came home with a different perspective and a much greater appreciation for what it meant to be American. I had also been studying abroad my junior year in college in Sydney, Australia, during 9/11 and being overseas when that happened was absolutely devastating. So, these two experiences of being abroad prompted me to look seriously into government service. I ended up going to the Defense Intelligence Agency through the Joint Military Intelligence College for my master's degree.

I was one of ten civilian students, and **it was truly a life changing experience to work so closely with active duty military and other government intelligence professionals**.

I always had a passion for Asian studies so going into the intelligence field with a focus on the Asia Pacific region made sense and I enjoyed the analytical work immensely. Since then, while I've done different things, I've always considered myself a lifelong intelligence analyst."

– *Suzanna Morrow*

"I grew up in South Florida, went to public school, and was raised by a single mother. My home life was difficult and I found positive distractions in school, work, and church communities. I did well in school but never thought of myself as particularly smart. I've always been analytical and loved the sciences and geometry – more abstract and logical reasoning. I lived in a highly diverse community, which heavily influenced my motivation to be bilingual, travel, and have a deeper immersive understanding of the world and culture.

During my sophomore year in college, **I witnessed a violent crime and helped identify the perpetrators**. A group of young men had indiscriminately targeted and beaten a homeless man. I was involved in a police chase and provided the information that led to the group's arrest. It was a wild, adrenaline-filled experience and I felt totally in my element. I felt fierce in a way I had known most of my life. I'd been fighting for my dignity and safety since I was young. I never thought this was unique, but the way the officers reacted made me think maybe it was. Maybe this is what I could offer the world and make a living doing as well. This is when I decided I wanted to become a special agent in the FBI. After college, I moved to Pittsburgh, then to Baltimore and eventually to Virginia, gradually working my way towards more opportunity in DC. I was offered a summer internship at Total Intelligence Solutions (TIS), one of the first boutique, third-party open source intelligence providers for the private sector. I worked full-time in Arlington, VA for no pay and waitressed at PF Changs at night to cover my expenses, driving back and forth from Baltimore every day. It was one of the hardest things I've ever done. After three months, I still had no job prospects and was about to give up on my dream of working for the government. Then, fortunately, in late summer, a LATAM Analyst role opened at TIS, and I was hired. I quickly took on the contract for a major agro-business as well. TIS was an incredible experience. It was there that I learned about the very real threats and vast risks to executives and companies, and how intelligence analysis could provide real value. In late 2010, the recession took its toll and TIS folded. Now with some experience under my belt, I had no trouble getting interviews with government agencies. I passed the FBI logic test and started the interview process with the CIA. However, government jobs and clearance work take a long time, and I needed paid work. I was offered a contract role for Microsoft in Ft Lauderdale, FL, near my immediate family. I took the job to get back to the sunshine and work until I got my clearance. I thought I would do it for just a while, but I ended up loving it and never looked back."

- Liz Maloney

"When I was 19, my uncle was kidnapped by Marxist-Leninist guerrillas in Colombia. I cycled back from a university lecture to find a note pinned to the post-room noticeboard at my Cambridge college: 'Rachel Briggs phone home urgently.' Those five words changed the course of my life, both personally and professionally.

I was thrown into a world of private sector negotiators, response consultants, and diplomats.

I learned the phrase 'proof of life' and consumed everything I could about Colombia. Until that point, I probably couldn't have located the country on a map. I coped with my fear and uncertainty by being organized, getting educated, and not talking to my friends about the drama that gripped my family back home. As I've come to understand, everyone copes with trauma differently. Seven and a half months later, as I backpacked around Greece on my Summer holiday, I took a phone call from my mum on a remote, windy island, reception cutting in and out, as I struggled to hear what she was saying. My uncle had been released. Normal life could resume. In many ways, normal life did resume: exams, boyfriends, jobs, houses, dogs. But it was never the same again. Two questions hung over me: how could this happen to an ordinary family like mine? And how could my uncle's kidnapping have been prevented? So began a 30-year journey through the security industry, via internships and think tanks, non-profits to support hostages and their families, and a long relationship with the corporate security community. I quickly realized that the security industry was the key to answering my second question, and a university dissertation helped me to answer the first. **I came into corporate security because I saw firsthand how much it matters; it's what stops people like my uncle being kidnapped, prevents unsafe counterfeit medicines from reaching patients, and reduces the impact of terrorist attacks at shopping malls. This has been my North Star for thirty years, and I'm proud of the progress I have seen within the industry."**

– Rachel Briggs

Lit from the Start

As far back as I can remember, I always wanted to be a gangster. – Henry Hill, Goodfellas

"After I left the Air Force, it was time to finish my degree. **I worked nights as a security guard at a construction site**. During downtime while making my rounds, I was able to complete my homework. When the building became occupied, I was there for the early arrivals, who got to know me well. I made sure there was fresh coffee brewing to greet them. The security director was also one of the early arrivals, and after several months, he offered me a job. I started working as an in-house cash vault security guard for United Bank of Arizona. Months later, I received a promotion, shortly after our company was purchased by Norwest Banks, where I served as the local security representative."

– Maria Dominguez

"My path to security was found through trial and error. My initial educational goals were in the science field.

> **I was determined to become a forensic scientist before anyone even knew what that job entailed.**

I managed to gain employment with the Virginia Department of Forensic Science while in college, and then I met organic chemistry. I quickly realized that I was much better at hands-on work than lab work, and I decided to change my major to Criminal Justice to pursue crime scene investigations. I'm pretty sure I was the only Criminal Justice major with a double minor in Chemistry and Biology. From there, I went into Law Enforcement, where I spent nineteen years, fourteen of which were as an investigator. Burnt out from the work, I needed a new challenge and entered the world of corporate security."

- Wendy Bailey

"My passion for criminology began with an internship at US Customs, where I worked on international drug trafficking cases. That experience hooked me, and **I knew I wanted to dedicate my career to protecting the U.S.** On a personal level, as a teenage mom, I faced challenges that pushed me to grow up fast and build a better life for my son. At twenty-two, I joined the FBI, where I spent ten years gaining diverse experience in small teams. After moving to the private sector, I continued to grow through volunteer work in the security industry, meeting amazing people and sharpening my skills. I've had the opportunity to work in physical security, intelligence, executive protection, and other aspects of the industry. My career has always been driven by a deep commitment to protect and serve, both personally and professionally."

- Kristin Lenardson

"From a young age, I've been an advocate for justice, which is probably why I studied Criminology and Criminal Justice full-time at the University of Maryland. During college, I also worked full-time for a large retail organization as a Loss Prevention Agent. **It was through my education, personal experiences, and several witnessed accounts that I quickly became more aware of the social/political injustices surrounding not only our criminal justice system, but also the stigmatization between blue collar crime vs. white collar crime.** After graduating, I became an internal fraud investigator and then transitioned into corporate security."

- Julia Sanya

"As a kid, I idolized *Inspector Gadget*[5] and spent hours chasing *Carmen Sandiego*[6] across pixelated globes, captivated by the thrill of solving puzzles and the continuous learning that came with it. My grandfather, a forensic pathologist, brought those fictional adventures to life. I remember listening, wide-eyed, as he talked about his work and wanted to understand the why behind the stories he told. One moment vividly shifted my perspective. Looking back, this is when I realized that I wanted to study crime and prevent it. That moment was the murder of Matthew Shepard, a college student beaten to death because he was gay. The gut punch and heartache I felt solidified my desire to spend my time helping to protect and support others, especially those most vulnerable. Motivated by this desire, I pursued academic studies focused on psychology and crime. While studying, my path took an unexpected but welcome turn when I applied for a Crime Analyst role within the Corporate Security department of a large financial institution. I got the job. At that

---

[5] *Inspector Gadget*, an animated television series created by Bruno Bianchi, Andy Heyward, and Jean Chalopin, follows the adventures of a bumbling cyborg detective equipped with high-tech gadgets, first aired in syndication in 1983. DIC Audiovisuel, *Inspector Gadget*, 1983–1986.

[6] *Where in the World Is Carmen Sandiego?*, computer game, developed and published by Brøderbund, first released in 1985. Although a fictional master thief and antagonist, Carmen Sandiego has become an iconic figure in educational gaming and popular culture. Her character challenged gender norms by positioning a woman as the central figure in a narrative about global intelligence, pursuit, and problem-solving.

time, **I didn't even realize roles like that existed within organizations**. The job demanded the same critical thinking and analytical rigor as my academic work, but it also involved a real-time application of problem-solving to protect people and assets. I saw it as a practical, impactful extension of my passion for understanding behavior and mitigating harm."

- Arian Avila

"I was born and raised in Romania, and in my early teens (after watching *The Silence of the Lambs* and *The X-Files*[7]), I decided that **I wanted to work for the FBI** - lesson learned here: inspiration can come from some pretty unexpected places!! Pretty bold dream for a kid living with her mom and grandma as a low-income family in Eastern Europe. After a few unexpected turns, I found myself with a degree in Intelligence Studies, an internship with the FBI (and if you were wondering, yes, I did cry tears of joy in my car, in the parking lot of the Cleveland FBI building on my first day) and ultimately a job in the security team at Bank of America."

- Andreea Patra

"As the child of hippies who was routinely taken to anti-war protests and peace rallies by her parents (I can sing ALL of Pete Seeger's protest anthems by heart), I somehow ended up in the U.S. Department of Defense in my first official security role. Looking back, it seems quite inevitable that I would end up in the U.S. intelligence community given my academic focus on narcotics and insurgency risks around the world, but as a student, **I'd planned to become a diplomat or work in international development**."

- Claire Campbell

---

[7] *The X-Files*, created by Chris Carter, aired on Fox from 1993 to 2002 (revived 2016–2018). The character Dana Scully, portrayed by Gillian Anderson, became an archetype for women in science and security fields, offering a model of intelligence, professionalism, and resilience. Research later confirmed this impact: The Geena Davis Institute on Gender in Media, *The Scully Effect: I Want to Believe... in STEM* (Los Angeles: Geena Davis Institute on Gender in Media, 2018), found that women who were regular viewers of *The X-Files* were more likely to express interest in STEM and law enforcement careers, directly citing Scully as inspiration.

"My mother is one of the most influential figures in my journey toward security and technology. As Chinese immigrants to the US, she and my father came here in pursuit of educational and job opportunities. During my childhood, she worked full-time as a receptionist at a doctor's office during the day. In the evenings, she pursued her master's degree in computer science, often taking me to school with her. She always wanted to ensure our family was financially secure, and she always encouraged my interest in technology to support my success. I will never forget hooking up our first computer to a television screen and, a few years later, getting our first personal computer, where I spent most of my time playing *Carmen Sandiego* and *Space Invaders*. Throughout my childhood—while I may not always have had the most forward fashion or popular toys—I almost always had access to technology, from Prodigy and AOL (with my *own* phone line to use it) to a top-of-the-line computer for school. This experience informed my eventual entrance into cybersecurity, fusing technology and geopolitics, while I pursued a degree at Georgetown University's School of Foreign Service. During my time there, two women professors influenced my career trajectory. One was a leading expert in Information Warfare, and I remember a time in class where a few of us were struggling to get our laptop to work. Several students went to get support from the IT team, but our professor deftly solved the problem by bypassing the login to get the device to work. To this day, I still don't know specifically how she did it, but knowing she could do this in under five minutes was a lightbulb moment. The second professor had contributed to the formation of the U.S. Secret Service's first forensic labs. The formative moment of her class was when she demonstrated how someone could recover data from various electronic media. As a student who had lost many papers to computer malfunctions (and knew many classmates who had as well), watching forensic recovery was yet another lightbulb moment. These experiences ignited my interest in cybersecurity.

The actions and influence of these women shaped my professional path in profound ways.

All of them demonstrated expertise, resilience, adaptability, and a willingness to grow through discomfort—valuable lessons that guided my career. One that has spanned roles at the Naval Criminal Investigative Service (NCIS), the Federal Bureau of Investigation (FBI) as a Booz Allen Hamilton contractor, Yahoo, and Capital One."

- Lillian Teng

Pranoti Surve on Reporter turned Security Analyst:

> The security industry was not a viable career or job for a girl from Mumbai, a city of 22 million people. In fact, at the time, it wasn't even a career or a job field at all, much less for a young, non-veteran Indian woman. **There were no role models or examples**. My grandfather thought I would be a lawyer. My father thought I would be an engineer. My friends thought I would be a politician. My grandmother knew I would be a rebel. My English teacher thought I was going to write books. I thought I would be a print news journalist. In 1998-99, the TV news scene exploded in India and journalists became household names. Reporting from the frontlines in war zones, telling important stories and writing exposés. Such an exciting time, and of course, I was going to be an investigative reporter. I got my very first gig in journalism out of sheer stubbornness. I went to the office of the newspaper I respected the most and sat in the waiting room until the News Editor gave me fifteen minutes. A whole day passed and eventually, at 9 p.m., a very confused editor finally asked who I was and gave me my fifteen minutes. Those fifteen minutes resulted in a headfirst rabbit-hole plunge into the world of organized crime and terrorism and ended in the book *Dongri to Dubai: Six Decades of the Mumbai Mafia*[8].
>
> As the book project was ending in 2008, I realised there was no

going back. Social media companies like Twitter (RIP) and Facebook (also, RIP) were born and they changed the face of journalism. Overnight, all print journalism went "digital" and whole stories became limited to 140 characters. But this isn't the story of the death (and subsequent resurrection) of investigative reporting. It's the story of how I came to be in the security industry. I realized that I was going to have to pivot, and it would have to be very quickly. I decided to get a master's degree and was accepted at the School of Oriental and African Studies in London. The day after I landed in London, on September 15, 2008, Lehman Brothers went bankrupt, triggering a global shockwave that history now knows as the 2008 Financial Crisis. **This reporter was on the frontlines watching the story unfold, not knowing it was going to kickstart her career**. A career not in journalism.

Whilst in London, I realized I had a very specific intersection of skills and drivers – an understanding of the intersection between organized crime and terrorism in South Asia (the theatre for a historic war against terrorism), the need to make money to provide for myself combined with the ability to work my socks off. I had three part-time jobs that leveraged this expertise while I was studying in London and I walked to all of them – from east London to the west, come hail, snow or rain: once even with a cast on my leg. In 2009, it was time to return to Mumbai. As a foreign student, my choices were difficult but straightforward – find someone to sponsor work authorization (potentially, an expensive wait) or return to India and compete with 1.4 billion people for a break in a place where I had the right to work. In December 2009, I chose the latter.

The global economy was still reeling. Banks all over the world were paying unprecedented fines. The median age of the population in India was 24 in 2010, my exact age that year. Imagine the number of job seekers. This is when I first became aware that all entry-level jobs needed a minimum of two-years' work experience. How does a fresh graduate show two years of work experience? **I was experiencing the classic chicken-and-egg problem and needed someone to take a chance on me.** I did what I knew best then. I became stubborn and persistent. I began sending cold emails and trawling company websites and LinkedIn (est. 2003). Meanwhile, the 2008 Financial Crisis brought unprecedented regulation to the financial sector. Unbeknownst to my naïve self, the financial sector did what it knew best, threw money at the problem and started to invest heavily in risk management. Finally in January 2010, someone who worked at Pinkerton at the time called me late one night. He and I had never met and didn't know each other, but he was the recipient of multiple cold emails from me. **A rank stranger called me to say that someone he knew was hiring for an analyst position at a financial institution in Mumbai** – the epitome of paying it forward. It was a trial position, and if it worked out, could turn into something, but no guarantees. Challenge accepted. Naturally. I interviewed for the role, and so it came to pass that on February 8, 2010, I started in my first-ever role as an intelligence analyst in the private sector. The beginning of countless adventures.

- *Pranoti Surve*

* * *

---

[8] Hussain Zaidi, *From Dongri to Dubai: Six Decades of the Mumbai Mafia* (New Delhi: Tranquebar Press, 2012).

There is no one way into this work. These stories offer a glimpse of the many winding ways one can enter the field. Whether sparked by global events, pop culture, personal experiences, or acts of curiosity, these origin stories demonstrate that inspiration and purpose can emerge from unexpected sources. As Lillian Teng described the pivotal moments when women shaped the direction of her career in ways she couldn't have predicted, every story shared in this book is a beacon, one we hope will cast camaraderie, inspiration, and a desire to carry the torch forward.

2

Navigating Entry and Career Advancement

B reaking into this field can feel daunting. Like many other industries, it comes with unfamiliar language, insider connections, and unspoken rules. But first, let's get one thing straight: **you belong here**, and there are ways to claim your space in it. Sometimes it's about sharpening your skills or figuring out how to tell your story in a way that resonates with hiring managers. Other times, it's knowing where to look, who to talk to, and how to tune out the self-doubt that creeps in along the way.

But getting your foot in the door is just the beginning. Once you're in, the question becomes: Where do you want to go next? Figuring that out isn't always straightforward. Sometimes growth means climbing the ladder. Other times, it means stepping sideways to build new skills, broaden your perspective, or open doors you didn't even know existed. And along the way, you'll almost certainly face challenges or situations that test your confidence.

But here's what's up: you have more power to shape your path than you might realize. Knowing your worth, being strategic about your next move, and learning how to turn setbacks into stepping stones are all part of building a career that works for you.

This chapter offers what we wish we had known when we were starting out, what we've learned — sometimes the hard way — and the strategies that helped us take those first steps and beyond. There's no magic formula. But there is power in shared experience. And sometimes, knowing where to start or knowing you're not the only one figuring it out can make all the difference.

Let's talk about how to get your foot in the door, how to keep walking through it, or, alternatively, how to build your own door.

Skillsets that Matter

There is a particular set of skills that consistently opens doors. Critical thinking, strong communication, and a relentless curiosity are foundational. Whether your focus is intelligence, cybersecurity, investigations, or physical security, success often hinges on your ability to solve problems, assess risks, and adapt in rapidly changing environments. Just as important are collaboration, discretion, and integrity. These qualities help build trust in developing partnerships and executing more efficiently, particularly in high-stakes crisis situations.

We asked: What competencies should we focus on mastering to be successful in the industry?

"Strong writing skills, executive presence and persuasion skills, business acumen that includes how to write a business case, analytical skills, organizational skills, being a good listener, critical thinking, and technical capabilities (I hired a Data Scientist so we would have predictive analytics and behavioral analysis capabilities)."

- Jessica Hern

"Empathy, listening, and communication are crucial skills to have."
- Maria Dominguez

"A successful security professional is a business enabler who instills a sense of peace in the people they advise and protect. While traits like competence, diligence, and efficiency will be well received in any industry or role, what will make you memorable and likely propel your success is having empathy, integrity, and being authentic. These characteristics don't just transcend industries and borders but will add texture and richness to your life's experience."

- *Janina Lincke*

"I think the only things that are vital are the will to learn fast, take in vast amounts of information you're able to make quick decisions about it, and communicate effectively. I've worked with people who've come into this field in all sorts of ways, with different degrees or job experiences, and those are the consistent qualities we need. But I would recommend continuing education and certifications throughout one's career, and there are lots of groups (AIRIP[9], OSAC[10], and others) that offer analytical training. I would also recommend that physical security professionals start getting more education on cyber threats if they haven't already, as threats are far more cross-sectional than they used to be."

- *Mary Hackman*

"For me, I think of the three C's: Critical thinking, Communication, and Collaboration. Critical thinking enables you to analyze complex situations, anticipate potential risks, and make informed decisions in uncertain situations. Communication ensures that your team, leaders, and partners clearly understand your insights and recommendations. And collaboration reminds us that security is never a solo effort: building strong relationships with colleagues and external stakeholders amplifies your impact and effectiveness."

- *Arian Avila*

---

[9] AIRIP (Association of International Risk Intelligence Professionals), a 501(c)(6) nonprofit founded in 2015, empowers risk-intelligence practitioners by connecting, developing, and engaging professionals across business, cybersecurity, reputation, physical security, and political risk sectors through training, networking, and professional development. See airip.org for more info.

[10] The U.S. Department of State's Overseas Security Advisory Council (OSAC) serves as a public-private partnership, strengthening security collaboration between the government and the private sector. Check out osac.gov for more info.

Peggy O'Neill Reflects on Skills Imperative to her Leadership Journey:

In my personal journey, I have relied on my resilience and determination. I believe that effective leaders demonstrate resilience in the face of challenges. Women leaders often have to overcome societal expectations or workplace barriers, which can make us even more determined to persevere and succeed, showing others how to handle setbacks with grace. Three skills that have been important in my journey as a leader are EQ, Risk Management, and Adaptability.

Empathy and Emotional Intelligence (EQ): Women often bring higher levels of empathy and emotional intelligence into leadership roles. This helps us understand the needs and challenges of our teams, which can lead to better communication and idea-sharing, ultimately driving innovation in both products and processes.

Risk Management: Women's leadership often involves a more calculated approach to risk-taking. We may carefully analyze potential risks and opportunities, balancing innovation with practicality, which leads to sustainable long-term growth and progress.

Adaptability: Women in leadership roles are adept at navigating changing environments, adjusting strategies quickly in response to shifting markets or new technology. This flexibility allows us to drive innovation in rapidly evolving situations.

- Peggy O'Neill

The Importance (or lack) of Certifications and Law Enforcement Backgrounds

While certifications and law enforcement experience can certainly be helpful, they aren't the only paths, as evidenced by what women shared in the first chapter of this book. Today's security industry values a range of experiences, perspectives, and skills that go far beyond traditional backgrounds. Reread chapter one for just a sample of the various possible paths and for inspiration on your envisioned journey.

Do Certifications Matter? What about a background in law enforcement?

"Historically, security teams were people with law enforcement backgrounds with a focus on physical security and investigations. And those things are still needed, but the role of security organizations has changed in recent years, and different skill sets and backgrounds are critical in addition to the more traditional areas. **I think skills matter more than certifications**. Things like executive presence, risk management, business acumen, business writing and communication, analytic processes, and a high degree of comfort with wide-ranging technologies, including AI, data analytics, and open-source listening tools, are critical in a security team today. However, some skills usually come about through experience in law enforcement, namely, interview skills."

- Jessica Hern

"While my law enforcement background is the foundation of my security career, some of the best security professionals I have worked with came to security through different paths. Security acumen and mindset can develop through many different experiences, and it is more important to have diversity in thought and background to build a well-rounded security organization. Certifications are a personal choice. I have secured various certifications throughout my career, but it was always with the intent to continue my development rather than to validate my experience. **Certifications can open**

doors when looking for opportunities in the security field, but should be balanced with other education, training, and experience."

– Wendy Bailey

"The necessity of certifications depends on the job. For those doing investigations or executive protection, yes. If you're an analyst, I think there are a lot of really good analytical training courses out there. And the more training and certifications you have, the better your CV looks. This said, I don't think they're a prerequisite for any of the jobs in my orbit – hard-working people can always get those along the way. **I think the most important thing to me is the network and security community that is full of people willing to help** and provide their expertise to each other at any time of day or night."

– Mary Hackman

"People tend to think of physical strength in security, but the reality is that it takes a person with interpersonal skills, soft skills, negotiation, business and financial acumen, strategic thinking, empathy, etc. These are transferable skills that can be brought over from various industries and backgrounds, not just law enforcement or the military."

– Gladis De Leon

Tips for Breaking into the Security Industry

"Pass on what you have learned". - Yoda

We asked our contributors one critical question about getting started: **What advice do you have for women breaking into the industry?**

"**I advise finding a mentor who will be your guide, your advocate, your truth teller, and your inspiration.** Listen carefully and with a truly open mind to their stories, advice, encouragement, and constructive criticism. You're not going to follow their path necessarily, but you can learn so much from the arc of their career.

A mentor does not have to be someone working in the security arena, but someone who is further along in their career journey, who has experienced ups and downs, and who has been resilient. You will also need to be resilient as there will be setbacks and disappointments. See those as learning opportunities where you can grow and course correct.

The value of grit and dogged determination cannot be overstated.

Do not try to go it alone. Not only will that make for a lonely career journey, but you will miss out on the joys and satisfaction of finding "your people." Always keep expanding your professional network. Don't think of it in a transactional way, but value it as a gift that will keep on giving. There is an old girls' network, just as there is an old boys' network. Both are not to be underestimated. Both have their place and a right to exist. Men are not the enemy; they are new professional colleagues and friends to cultivate.

Don't simply keep your head down and concentrate on doing your job well. Of course, your employer may like that, but you will be selling yourself short. Seek out stretch roles and special projects that move you outside your comfort zone and test you in new ways. Allow yourself to be less than perfect and, at the same time, stop apologizing and explaining. Perfection is the enemy of accomplishment and happiness.

Explore new opportunities and career avenues even if you're completely happy with your current role. There's no harm in listening and it will make you examine, and perhaps rethink, your current course. If you chose not to make a change, that's fine, but you will be making a more informed choice.

Prioritize time with family and friends to maintain a healthy attitude about work and life. The work will always be there, but those you love may not be. Never forget that time is our most precious nonrenewable resource."

— *Kathy Lavinder*

"Don't worry about getting the first job you find in this industry; take that first opportunity to learn about the organizations in the public, private, and humanitarian sector without being beholden to one organization, brand, or various legal restrictions. **Investigate any job prospect like it is a reputational risk inquiry:** do you want to be associated with this organization on its bad day? Ask for informational meetings with members you find on LinkedIn or through other social media outlets, and if you are interviewing, ask for a one-on-one with team members so that you can see what the team dynamics are like. One colleague took this advice and found out in her job interview that half the security team had suffered, mentally and physically, from the erratic hours and an overbearing manager - **you want to break into the industry and not let the industry break you!** As you uncover the area in which the organization works, look at how many women are in that division. Are you willing to be a trailblazer? Are you going to have similar faces around the table when you need to direct a program or operation in a particular direction, with little time or little notice? I have often been in work environments where women account for less than 20% [of the staff], especially in security. **As a strong female leader, don't worry about being louder than the team; be precise and deliberate.** Your expertise will serve you more in the long term. **Take the odd tasks when you are new to your role.** These will introduce you to more people in the broader team and expose you to other skills you may need to develop. Taking on these side projects has also given me opportunities like travel, offers to join other teams, and career advancement."

- Tiffany Harbour

"Ask your leaders for opportunities to take on new assignments that will enhance your existing skills and provide exposure to different functions. **Be candid about what you are looking for upfront but keep an open mind and be flexible.** When you receive an offer, look at the whole picture and the future growth opportunities so you don't find yourself boxed in. Employers are looking for people who can bring diverse and new ideas to the table, and the best way to expand your knowledge is to talk to others who have been where you have been or faced some of the same challenges. You never know who you may need to call in the future, so try to cultivate these relationships once formed, even if it's just an annual check-in."

- Haylea Parkes

"Don't be afraid to approach others to build your network. Network with women in security but also men in the industry who can be your promoters and sponsors. I obtained a great role by someone reaching out to me, telling me they thought I would click well with the hiring manager. She was correct! While I don't work there anymore, my former manager and I are good friends. Also, **never turn down the opportunity to speak to a recruiter** – but be honest! I have told recruiters who have reached out to me that I would love to speak to them about the role, but that I'm not actively looking, happy at my current company, etc. Almost in every instance, the recruiter still wanted to speak and keep in touch in case another opportunity arose. In one instance, the recruiter convinced me to leave, although I had no plans to leave. It was a unique opportunity that allowed me to grow in my career – one I would not have known of if I hadn't kept the lines of communication open."

- *Gladis De Leon*

Lillian Teng Drops Knowledge from Experience:

A Closed Mouth Never Gets Fed. My senior year at Georgetown coincided with the events of September 11th. Watching the smoke float off the Pentagon, hearing rumors flying across DC of additional attacks, and having multiple friends and classmates terrified for families across Manhattan, shook the security and foundation for many of us. And while Georgetown is known for its graduates entering public service, this event sparked even greater interest in serving in government. Like many, I applied across the government with an eye towards working in computer forensics (now called host-based forensics within cyber) for the US government.

After graduation I worked for several non-profits in information technology roles, but then received an offer from the NCIS to become a Special Agent. In January 2003, I packed my bags and headed to Glynco, Georgia to attend a 17-week training program at FLETC, the Federal Law Enforcement Training Center. There I would learn all of the fundamental skills to become a criminal investigator, followed by seven weeks of training specific to working within the Department of the Navy. When I signed my job offer, I was told that, due to my Foreign Service background, I was assigned to join the counterintelligence program. And while I was happy to do so, I asked if there was a possibility of going to the Computer Investigations and Operations unit instead. Unfortunately, there were no available spots. Upon graduation from FLETC, I was posted to the Washington DC field office. Throughout my time at FLETC, I maintained my interest in cyber and continued to inquire about opportunities. Being vocal (and patient) paid off! After my first week in the field office, I was reassigned to the Computer Investigations and Operations (CIO) department, as there was a CIO Agent who wanted to swap to counter-intelligence. This experience is one of many, which prompts me to always tell people not to be afraid to ask for what they want.

Your Career is a Jungle Gym, Not a Ladder. The misconception that career growth is a straightforward, upward trajectory is limiting. While it is always important to set goals, it's less important to set prescriptive ways to achieve them. Give yourself grace to deviate from your "plan." Life and circumstances change, your plan is allowed to as well.

In my career, I have taken a few "resets," the first occurred after leaving NCIS. While I enjoyed my time there, I spent four years of my eight-year tenure overseas and by the latter point in my time I had gotten married, and the choices impacted more than just myself. My spouse also worked for the government, but at the beginning of our marriage, in a country twelve hours away. After a year of being apart, he left his position to join me in Japan. We likely could have continued to travel and move throughout the work, but with five overseas moves under our collective belts, we decided it was time to leave government service. This pause enabled me to assess what my priorities were for my next opportunity. Ultimately, I ended up joining Booz Allen Hamilton and going back into government service as a contractor for the FBI, supporting the National Cyber Joint Investigative Task Force (NCIJTF) and the FBI Asia Cyber Operations division. While this role appeared very similar to the one I left, I was able to leverage this opportunity to gain skills I would otherwise not have access to in the government and obtain a work-life balance that was missing.

The Booz Allen role often felt like adopting two different identities, one on client-site where I was supporting FBI Cyber agent cases and investigations, the other my Booz Allen persona as an associate focused on business development. Additionally, I was a people leader for the first time, managing an amazing Booz Allen team supporting FBI Cyber. This dual identity enabled me to continue to hone my cyber expertise and learn about the business aspects of Booz Allen. But after several years and a promotion, I realized this was not where my passions lie.

At this point, I came across an opportunity at Yahoo to join and help build up their team to protect their customers against government-backed attackers. I left FBI/Booz Allen in 2016, right as Yahoo announced the largest breach in history. And for the first time, I was working in the real private sector, without the safety net of government contracts and the environment I had spent most of my career in. This move felt like I went from leading a team at Booz Allen, back to an individual contributor position.

Growth Lies on the Other Side of Discomfort. If you are not uncomfortable, you're probably not growing. And to be clear, I do not mean tolerating toxic situations. What I mean here is that you should be willing to take risks!

When NCIS asked me to take an independent duty position in Bahrain, I was terrified. I had never lived on my own overseas and I certainly had never been on my own as a cyber agent. But in taking that one year position, I learned so much professionally and personally, that when an opportunity to take a role in Japan came up, it did not feel as "risky" and I was able to take the leap.

Later in my career, I felt similar discomfort leaving the security of the US government sphere to join Yahoo. Yahoo was a completely different environment; there were no longer prescriptive playbooks or policies to follow, as many of the attacks and activities observed on the platform were novel. We were faced with dedicated human adversaries, later disclosed to be the Russian Federal Security Service (FSB), and working with some of the most insightful and dedicated colleagues within the Yahoo Paranoids (as the cybersecurity team was called), we often had to collaborate across the company to make the right decisions for our users.

I learned a lot in my time at Yahoo. I eventually transitioned from being an individual contributor on my team to a people leader, and learned skills such as holding difficult conversations with kindness and candor and was empowered to taking risk, such as hiring those who didn't necessarily have the "perfect" cyber experience (like the US government did for me out of college!). I had to learn to understand problems from so many different perspectives due to our global customer base. After a few years, I was promoted to a Director, leading multiple teams tackling adversaries targeting all of Yahoo customers.

Put Your Mask on First. This is a piece of advice that is given over and over and over again, no matter what field you are in. And in security it is absolutely vital. Depending on where you may be in cyber, you may deal with traumatic events or content which can and will weigh on you. Focusing on your health and mental well-being and not being afraid to seek help is the only way to build resilience. In security, we are taught to be "tough" and often turn to unhealthy coping mechanisms. But those short-term mechanisms harm us in the long run. Setting boundaries and learning healthy resilience practices are key to avoiding burnout.

- *Lillian Teng*

"The journey through a professional career can be quite a rollercoaster. Taking a step back can often provide the perspective needed to come back stronger and more resilient. **Do not fear setbacks** or be concerned about titles or the absence of a team, even if you have previously held a managerial position. Focus on the long-term perspective rather than the immediate situation. Every experience, whether positive or negative, is valuable."

- *Maria Stone*

"As you gain experience and learn how to do your job, **benchmark yourself against your peers across your network**. You will know if you're undervalued or not, and if you are, it's probably going to fall to you to correct that. Talk to your manager about your compensation, level, and title, and test the market now and then. Speak to recruiters, talk to leaders who know your industry, look at job descriptions, and make sure you understand what your fair market value is. There are so many resources available to educate yourself if you are getting ready to push for increased scope, different responsibilities, a promotion or raise, or if you're about to interview for a new role. Once you get a few wins under your belt, it gets easier. And if you still don't have confidence in your value and you still have a seed of doubt in your mind, **find someone who will advocate for you**. In my 20+ years as an intelligence professional, I've been a people manager for about nine years. My own experience has been that men never fail to ask for promotions, while women almost never bring it up. It's my job as a manager and mentor to coach others to help them build their confidence and improve their performance while advocating for them. If your manager doesn't do that for you, go find someone who will. And when you become the person who can assess talent and speak for others, lean into that role and go be that mentor for the next generation."

- *Suzanna Morrow*

If Only I Knew Then What I Know Now

"I wish I could go back to the beginning of the season, put some money on the Cubbies" - Old Terry, Back to the Future Part II

We asked contributors: What do you wish you had known when starting in the security industry?

"I wish I had understood **the importance of networking, mentoring, and sponsorships**—not to wait for them to happen but to actively pursue them. To succeed, you need someone to propel you forward and help you along the way. It is possible to succeed without these supports, but it typically takes longer, and your progress may be limited."

- Maria Dominguez

"I was ill-prepared for the challenges I would face as a woman in a male-dominated industry, not because I was naive, but because I was raised to believe there were no limits on what I could do. I don't think it would have dissuaded me, but **going in with an understanding of how my gender would predefine my abilities for many of my peers would have better prepared me for the challenges**. I quickly found a female mentor who had faced the same challenges and helped me understand how to navigate the boys' club. She told me, "You have to work twice as hard and be twice as good, but only expect half the credit." Thankfully, there has been a positive shift in how women are respected in security since I started my career, but there are still areas for improvement."

- Wendy Bailey

"Being smart, curious, bold, dogged, charismatic, confident, a good writer, and ambitious will get you a long way, and you should never let anyone make you feel you aren't any of those things – you'll need those qualities your whole career. This said, in a heavily male-dominated field, it's likely you'll encounter positions or roles where your voice is less heard, and **I wish I could go back**

and stay for less time in those positions. Not every situation is one where you can just do all the right things and be assured that the situation will change. Now I try my best to be in places where my skills are appreciated and valued instead of trying so hard to fit in. I have also learned over time **to pace myself better**. The security field is a series of managing one crisis after another, and slowing down, taking deep breaths, and incorporating self-care is incredibly important to maintaining the balance needed – it actually makes me better at handling the crises well when they do arrive."

- *Mary Hackman*

"**It's not only okay, but important to be you**. There was no amount of trying to be one of the guys that was going to make me fit in. Let your uniqueness be an avenue to visible authenticity, and let that visibility shine a light on why you are a trusted and critical component of the team. For me this meant learning to be okay with not having the professional experience or academic credentials that many of my peers had but knowing that my grit and feeling okay not knowing it all allowed me to work without the creative limitations that others put on themselves."

- *Jennifer Walters*

> **It's not what you know, it's who you know** and whether they take your call or reply to your text when it matters. You cannot know everything.
>
> **Prioritize long-term respect over short-term liking**, the former outlives the latter. You can't win life's popularity contest every day, but if you continue to hone your professional craft and conduct yourself with integrity, you will perceive your interpersonal outcomes are higher in quality because they're based on respect.
>
> **There's no replacement for drive and a focus on improving your ways of working**. None. The will to keep going and become a better version of yourself trumps all. Sooner or later, the barriers will come crashing down.

As time passes, focus and intentionality become crucial in maintaining the quality of life that births satisfaction and contentment. If you allow yourself to remain on life's conveyor belt without challenging your mind, you will find yourself adrift or bored, or both at once.

It's okay to change your mind about the source of your fulfilment; what worked for you once may not be the thing that sparks joy for you forever.

Shut out the noise generated by your detractors. In life, as in security, negative behaviors originating from biases will manifest in many different forms, but usually they boil down to insecurity (you're too competent) or jealousy (you're too young to have this so soon). Eventually, those who ignore excellence do so at their peril.

However, your detractors are not always wrong. They often see your weaknesses more clearly than you do because they fixate on them, while you fixate on your strengths. If you pay attention to your detractors, you might just figure out what you can do better and then be able to fix it.

Build the bridge, and the marchers will come. If you ever find yourself excluded, create your own tribe. You are not alone on a planet of eight billion people; you couldn't possibly be.

Care, be vulnerable, and prepared to give more than you receive. In turn, you will find you are enriched more than you imagined, and certainly more than you would be if you sought out more than you were willing to give of yourself.

Never forget where you came from. Your roots and every fork in your life's journey have contributed to making you who you are. And they will form the basis for who you become and the story you will tell about yourself.

- Pranoti Surve

We asked: What experiences have you had with moving to different parts of the business outside of security and what did you learn?

"I once transitioned from the Physical Security field to Cybersecurity. Although I did not enjoy it as much as my prior roles in Physical Security, I gained significant knowledge and, more importantly, realized how much I missed the Physical Security field and my professional colleagues and friends. **Returning to Physical Security was challenging, and I had to accept several roles that were not my ideal jobs.** However, these roles set me on the right path and enabled me to return to the field I am passionate about, stronger and more determined than ever."

- Maria Stone

"One of the most important career choices I made was to leave my role as Chief of Staff/Director of Strategic Planning for the Chief Security Officer at Disney to be the Chief of Staff/Director of Strategic Operations for the Chief Technology Officer at Disney Parks/Experiences. It was a lateral move - no increase in pay or title - but it was a critical pivot to show that my business operations and organizational development skills were transferable beyond my security expertise. **I had literally ZERO technology experience beyond working with our security systems teams, and no knowledge of mobile apps or product management; but I knew how to align an organization behind a business strategy and make its design, processes, and culture work towards priority business outcomes.** This move gave me two years of C-suite-level tech and digital experience and solidified my ability to fully pivot away from the silo of "only a security executive" to "a business performance and culture leader" - far more valuable to my long-term career than any salary or title bump.

- Jessica Martinez

"I was tapped to lead a Reporting function, which challenged me to the core as it meant a move away from Security. **Sometimes we confuse our identity with our jobs, which prevents people from being open to new opportunities and experiences.** Making this move gave me more confidence than I could have imagined. It was ultimately the stepping stone that allowed me to leap to another company altogether."

- Arian Avila

Leadership roles tend to bring a different set of challenges. We asked: As folks move into more senior roles, what should they consider?

"One of the biggest mistakes I see security leaders making again and again is **assuming that everyone shares their belief that security is THE most important priority in the business**. For better or worse, it's simply not true and for many businesses; they are not in a financial or organizational position to invest in or prioritize the zero-risk solution.

Take security awareness. During my time at Disney, this became one of our top priority solutions to help both prevent and respond to threats and crises across the company; however, many teams around the world weren't interested in security awareness communications or trainings. They didn't feel the risk was as high, and given so many other business priorities, they didn't want to add noise to their employee messaging or add on time-intensive trainings that took away from value-added work. Instead of forcing it on them over email from LA, we flew to them in their local office and met them face to face. In one specific instance, we flew to our offices in Warsaw, Poland. We spent the time with them learning about their local business and teams, and listening to their concerns, even if they didn't align with our thinking. Then we left. No hard sell. No 'You have until this date to do this.' We simply thanked them, and over the next few months, I'd send emails intermittently giving them a quick update on what we'd been up to with no call-to-action. Eventually - in less than three months - they actually responded with a request. "We're seeing a higher incidence of bike accidents. Is this something you could help with?" Admittedly, not really our scope, but yes - we'd help them. We created posters with biking safety and security tips, an email campaign, and even ordered glow in the dark bracelets for riders. It was low cost, highly effective, and most importantly, demonstrated to the local team that we had value to offer them as partners. Almost immediately, they bought into the rest of our security awareness messaging.

The key takeaway for me was **that building partnerships and alliances will always be about listening and serving, not dictating and selling. When you take the time to build the trust and demonstrate value, the partnership will always follow.**"

- Jessica Martinez

"Read the book *What Got You Here Won't Get You There*[11]. Basically, what made you successful in an individual contributor or middle management role isn't going to make you successful at the more senior, executive levels. The work is less about managing incidents in the moment and more about shaping the environment that prevents them, anticipating risk before it materializes. Impact needs to come through influence, by building trust, aligning stakeholders, and translating security needs into the language of business. **Investing in mentorship, amplifying diverse voices, and deliberately creating pathways for your team become central responsibilities.** Perhaps most importantly, stepping into senior leadership calls for thinking beyond the present moment and toward legacy."

- Arian Avila

* * *

---

[11] Marshall Goldsmith with Mark Reiter, *What Got You Here Won't Get You There: How Successful People Become Even More Successful* (New York: Hyperion, 2007).

Breaking into the security industry and moving around can feel like stepping into the unknown, but the voices shared in this chapter remind us we're not alone. No matter where you are starting from, be that another industry, a career pivot, a classroom, or just a deep sense of purpose, know that there's room for you here. As you take your next step, remember that the light you carry will help someone else find their way, too.

II

Thriving in the Field

3

Finding Your Voice, Building Your Brand, and Dealing with that B*tch (Imposter Syndrome)

For many women entering the security industry, the image of Jodi Foster as Clarice Starling in *The Silence of the Lambs*[12] resonates. Being one of the few, or the first, can be isolating, intimidating, and exhausting. Plus, for many of us, the idea of self-promotion feels uncomfortable and self-serving.

We've been taught to keep our heads down, let our work speak for itself, and avoid "bragging." But here's the reality: in a competitive, fast-paced field like security, quietly doing great work isn't always enough. If people don't know what you bring to the table, they might overlook you entirely.

Building your professional brand isn't about ego. It's about visibility, opportunity, and ensuring your story isn't written for you. It's knowing how to highlight your strengths, share your achievements, and connect with others in a way that's authentic and genuine.

---

[12] *The Silence of the Lambs*, directed by Jonathan Demme (1991; Burbank, CA: Orion Pictures, 2001), DVD. Clarice Starling, portrayed by Jodie Foster, is often cited as a groundbreaking fictional representation of a woman in law enforcement and security, challenging gender stereotypes in a traditionally male-dominated field.

Like Clarice, women in this field are not just surviving the system; they are reshaping it and thriving. What follows are *vocal lanterns* of those who've stepped into that space, offering insights, encouragement, and hard-earned wisdom for those who are ready to do the same.

We asked: How have you found your voice?

"Finding my professional voice has, and likely will continue to be, an ever-evolving journey. I have been very fortunate to have a series of incredibly supportive managers who encouraged me to share my thoughts and perspectives and allowed me to take ownership of programs, projects, and teams. I think as women, we are often given a lot of advice on how to communicate in the corporate space, and honestly, I have ignored it all. **I simply cannot be anything else than genuine – I just can't do anything except care about my work and care about the people around me, and lead from the heart.** It sounds cliché, but I don't know how else to put it. I am absolutely awkward at times, but you are always getting my real reactions and feelings. Now that being said, a lot of my communication style comes from my training as a teacher, and my time working in crisis management. I always approach all communication from the perspective of trying to get the individuals or groups to a place of alignment. I'm also fiercely protective about ensuring I don't let my own feelings or bad days trickle down onto those around me. If I'm struggling, I would rather be open and honest about it with my peers and team than try to hide it and end up acting in ways that are detrimental to the team."

- Alyssa Nayyar

"It took me time to cultivate my voice and approach when communicating to both teammates and partners. I've been called a 'bubbly person' with 'high energy' and 'always smiling.' And while those can be considered compliments, those personality traits can make it challenging to be taken seriously in our field. **I find that emulating the leadership of someone well-regarded in your organization is a great way to gain trust, such as using similar vocabulary or employing terminology found within the company's internal**

communications, for example. I take a minute to prepare for calls and meetings so that while I may be seen as cheerful and willing to partner, I also know my material and will advocate for my desired outcomes. I'm very upfront about admitting if I don't have subject matter expertise in an area of discussion – I will not dance around that. It takes some humility, but I've also learned to cull my written communications down. I love to write and send really detailed emails, but I know that not everyone responds well to large blocks of a narrative, nor does everyone have time to read lengthy notes. Lastly, while I am passionate about security, I learned a long time ago that not everyone is, nor do organizations necessarily put security at the front and center of their plans. Be willing to compromise on the smaller stuff and gain a reputation for being someone great to work with – then when you do need to dig in, your insistence will carry more weight, and hopefully get the buy-in that you need!"

- Elena Carrington

"Finding my voice was an evolving process. Early in my career, I struggled with speaking up, doubting my knowledge and experience, especially in rooms where I was the only woman. Through experiences, I discovered what my personal brand really is, whether that involves creating long-term execution focused strategies, being an effective change agent and leader, or operating as a process-driven work environment champion. Since then, my voice has focused on advancing and championing the personal brand, despite obstacles, challenges or workplace dynamics. **I started by contributing in smaller ways—asking thoughtful questions, preparing for meetings in advance, having an ally or mentor review my plans ahead of speaking up, and ensuring that my ideas were well-researched.** I also emphasize that purpose-driven life has been a key element of my personal brand and my voice wasn't just about myself—it was about lifting others as well. Whether leading by example, mentoring professionals, or challenging unfair assumptions, I discovered empowerment in my own voice when it was used to lift others up."

- Sweta Patel

"As I've grown, I've learned that knowing when to speak up is just as important as knowing when to stay quiet. There are moments when your voice adds value, offering insights, solutions, or perspectives that can drive progress. But just as vital is the ability to recognize when to hold back, resisting the urge to offer your two cents just for the sake of speaking. Moreover, it's important to hold space for others' contributions as well. **True contribution comes not from filling every silence, but from discerning when your words will make the most impact.**"

— *Angela Lewis*

"As a first-generation American child of immigrants, English was my second language, and it was incredibly challenging to find a voice in a country I barely understood in childhood. Not only was I attempting to translate the world for myself, but I was also doing so for my parents. As my English developed and surpassed that of my parents, **I understood that I needed to be clear, direct, honest, and respectful to communicate effectively with different audiences**. I've used this in my interactions across life. I've used my voice to help others find theirs and to share messages within my sphere of influence: by bringing people to the table who didn't originally have a seat, sharing my own lessons learned, influencing new decisions, creating ideas, and supporting hobbies and charities of diverse backgrounds. All of these things come together to show people that you're listening, they matter, and it creates a level of trust for them to share more."

— *Olga Kocharyan*

We asked: What communication techniques have worked for you?

> Assertiveness from women is often received differently than assertiveness from men; learning how to assert without triggering negative reactions is a critical skill. Eliza Van Court, in her book,

A Woman's Guide to Claiming Space: Stand Tall. Raise Your Voice. Be Heard[13] provides insights on how women can use their voice effectively:

1. Participate in meetings early, speaking within the first five to ten minutes.
2. Do not shrink yourself through posture or minimizing language such as uptalk or over-apologizing.
3. Speak clearly, directly, and confidently. You can command authority without speaking loudly.

"**The most powerful communication tool is active listening**. This helps tailor responses ensuring customer satisfaction, builds trust in the system and learning about your audience. Storytelling has been another impactful way of communication, especially when security professionals often have to emphasize the importance of safety to senior leaders and stakeholders. **Using real-world scenarios, analogies, and metrics helps make security concerns more relatable to non-security stakeholders**. Being clear and concise, especially when security professionals often work under high pressure is important. Getting straight to the point while providing key details builds credibility."

- *Sweta Patel*

"My communication style leans towards the direct kindness side with a mix of "treat others how you would like to be treated". *Respect is the best tool.* **Approach conversations with positive intent**, assume the same from the receiving end, and understand the purpose of a conversation is to come to a mutual understanding, not a mutual agreement, of information exchanged.

---

[13] Eliza VanCort, A Woman's Guide to Claiming Space: Stand Tall. Raise Your Voice. Be Heard (Oakland, CA: Berrett-Koehler Publishers, 2021).

The information exchange will ultimately influence how you make decisions and will reflect the progress in the conversation. When you realize most people are just out here living their life the best way they can, it becomes easier to look at it as a person-to-person exchange rather than "what can ONLY I get out of this?" If a conflict arises, address it directly and as soon as possible. Time only allows the problem to fester. Nip animosity in the beginning and work on rebuilding the respect for each other."

— Olga Kocharyan

"Working in international settings, I believe multilingual people tend to communicate more clearly with other cultures. While it is not an easy task to pick up a new language, it is a good idea to **pay attention to the way these people address a group of people**, speaking clearly, avoiding cultural references, looking at the audience to make sure they are following along, nodding and giggling where appropriate. I think it's a good idea to do some research on a location before traveling there. Be prepared to adapt to new cultures with open eyes and respect."

— Eva Deren

"I have always valued kindness and manners, which translates to **paying attention to who is in the room**. I do, however, have to carry an imaginary swear jar with me at all times. Less is more, if you can explain something in one sentence, great, no need for embellishment."

— Michelle Rowe

Why should you be intentional about your brand?

> **Pro Tip:** Build visibility and credibility by taking on impactful work outside of your current scope. If you can't find these opportunities within your specific team or company, seek opportunities within an industry association. Join or create a women's network within your

company. Find opportunities to speak at events, individually or as part of a panel, and share your expertise and insights.

"Merriam-Webster and I agree on the definition of intentional— "not accidental." By that definition, I live my life with intention. To me, being intentional means living with purpose, not leaving things to chance. It's no accident that I work hard to become the best version of myself. My brand is me. My brand is a reflection of who I am—my name, my reputation, and the integrity I bring to both my personal and professional life. Every day, I ask myself: Am I trustworthy? Am I honorable? Do people have confidence in me? These questions guide my choices and my relationships.

Building a brand isn't about self-promotion—it's about alignment. I've built mine through consistency, hard work, and staying true to the values I was raised with: honesty, humility, reliability, and ethical behavior. Mistakes happen, of course, but I strive to learn from them and grow. In doing so, my brand evolves in a way that reflects both who I am and who I aim to be. I work hard to be the best version of myself every day: To be honest, trustworthy, giving, reliable, hardworking, and ethical are the traits I value and espouse. Using these as my north star makes me successful."

- Dorian Van Horn

"Being intentional about your brand matters because **if you don't define it for yourself, others will define it for you**. Your brand is not just your resume or LinkedIn profile...it is the consistent story people tell about who you are, how you lead, and the value you bring. It's what they say about you when you're not in the room. In security, where trust, credibility, and influence are essential, an intentional brand helps you stand out, build authority, and open doors to new opportunities. It allows you to align how you are perceived with how you want to be perceived, ensuring that your voice, your values, and your impact are recognized."

- Arian Avila

How do you identify the right writing and speaking opportunities?

"I gravitate toward interactive engagements—ones that foster real dialogue rather than traditional lectures. Early on, I struggled with the pressure of being the "expert in the room". The first time my college roommate asked me to speak to her class, I was terrified and got caught up in my own thoughts about it. I tried to be an expert lecturer, but it didn't go well until I relaxed and just behaved like myself. That experience taught me that authenticity matters more than perfection. When I stopped trying to perform and shared what I knew, I connected more deeply with audiences. It was okay that I didn't have all the answers to the questions. I realized each of us has something to bring to the table, and no one is expected to bring everything. When evaluating opportunities to speak or write, I try to identify which opportunities fit me best. I ask myself a few key questions:

- Do I have something of value to share?
- Who is the audience?
- Will this be collaborative or interactive?
- What impact can I make?

It is similar to writing. I ask myself what I have to offer. Writing is still a skill I'm honing. I've learned to tailor my approach depending on the audience—whether it's a formal report or a piece for publication. My goal is always to inform, engage, and add meaningful value."

- Dorian Van Horn

"I find that the most effective opportunities are those that align with both my expertise and the audience's interests or needs. I consider **impact over visibility**. Not every platform or event is worth the time; I prioritize venues where I can genuinely influence thinking, spark dialogue, or provide actionable guidance. This might be a conference where my insights help shape industry practices (like mental health awareness), a panel that elevates underrepresented voices (like Global Security Pride), or an article that contributes meaningfully to ongoing conversations in security or leadership (like on emerging trends or forecasting). I also evaluate **fit with my brand and values**. Speaking and writing engagements should reinforce the story I want to tell about my expertise and perspective. If an opportunity doesn't align with my values, goals, or the audience I serve, I pass. Part of identifying the right engagements is also **being intentional with my time**. Even when an opportunity is appealing, I have to weigh it against current priorities to ensure I'm able to give it the focus and energy it deserves. These engagements take a lot of mental energy! I make it a practice to thank those who think of me, acknowledge the value of the opportunity, and, if the timing isn't right, politely decline while expressing interest for future consideration."

- Arian Avila

How do you balance humility with giving yourself space to shine?

"Each night, I reflect on the day and ask: Did I contribute something meaningful? If the answer is yes, then I feel I've had a bright and successful day. I don't seek the spotlight, but I do believe in stepping up when needed—and in owning my contributions. When someone recognizes me for a job well done, I am truly grateful. It reinforces that I am indeed doing what I set out to do, the right thing. It is OK to take credit for my hard work. It's essential to recognize the hard work, grit, and innovation that contribute to success. At the same time, I never forget that meaningful accomplishments are rarely the result of solo efforts. "One team, one fight" is a mantra I live by. Staying humble is keeping that focus on the team, bringing others along, honoring everyone along the way, and yes, accepting the honor of a job well done."

- Dorian Van Horn

"Over the years, I've benefited from mentors (and hired a coach!) to help me own my dopeness. Early in my career, I measured myself against other people's ideas of branding/credibility/success, and it took some time for me to believe that I could be true to myself while aggressively (yeah, I said it) advancing my career. With that self-awareness, it's easy to say yes to things that excite or challenge me and say no to things that aren't in line with my values and goals.

> **Understanding that not everything is a fit for me - and I'm not a fit for everyone either - keeps me focused on opportunities that matter to me.**

I feel fortunate to be in a place where I can use my credibility as a platform to support other women, which I see as a collective responsibility. If I may offer advice to our community, I would recommend taking risks, forging your own path, and being willing to walk away from anything that is not bringing you closer to who/what you want to be."

- Lianne Boudali-Kennedy

"I balance humility and visibility by owning my contributions without overshadowing others. I give credit where it's due, listen actively, and share my expertise when it adds value. Humility doesn't mean hiding your light...it means shining in a way that lifts everyone around you. The key is framing your accomplishments in a way that benefits others, whether it inspires your team, educates your peers, or advances an initiative. This way you highlight what you bring to the table while remaining grounded in gratitude and respect for those around you."

- Arian Avila

We wanted to know: How do you deal with that b*tch IMPOSTER SYNDROME?

> Imposter syndrome is the persistent feeling of self-doubt or inadequacy despite clear evidence of competence and success. Psychologists Pauline Clance and Suzanne Imes first identified the phenomenon in high-achieving women in 1978[14]. It often leads

people to attribute accomplishments to luck or fear being "found out" as less capable than they are.

In male-dominated fields like security, imposter feelings can be heightened. Recent research confirms these experiences are not a reflection of actual ability, but rather a response to systemic barriers, cultural stereotypes, and underrepresentation.[15] For women in security, imposter syndrome can show up as questioning belonging in the field, even as if contributions prove otherwise.[16]

"It never goes away! **When I start feeling like this I try and focus on the progress I have made** and try and see myself through the eyes of others who support and believe in me. Distraction is another good way to deal with the feelings - distract yourself with some other task and the feelings will fade."

- Haylea Parkes

"I definitely have dealt with imposter syndrome! There will always be someone who knows more or is an expert in an area you are not. **Instead of feeling intimidated, get to know them, ask them for guidance, information, best practices et**c. I've never had someone turn down a request for assistance. They are happy to mentor me, even if informally."

- Gladis De Leon

"I've also wrestled with imposter syndrome. It's a natural feeling—especially in a field where the stakes are high and there's little room for error. A single misstep could mean a criminal walks free or a family is denied justice. But I

---

[16] Pauline R. Clance and Suzanne A. Imes, "The Imposter Phenomenon in High Achieving Women: Dynamics and Therapeutic Intervention," *Psychotherapy: Theory, Research & Practice* 15, no. 3 (1978): 241–247.

[16] Dena M. Bravata et al., "Prevalence, Predictors, and Treatment of Impostor Syndrome: A Systematic Review," *Journal of General Internal Medicine* 35 (2020): 1252–1275.

[16] Ruchika Tulshyan and Jodi-Ann Burey, "Stop Telling Women They Have Imposter Syndrome," *Harvard Business Review*, February 11, 2021.

remind myself that **my credibility wasn't given; it was earned**. I have years of hands-on experience. I've built systems, responded to real cases, and trained others in the field. I'm a seasoned professional who understands the gravity of the work—and I continue to show up with both humility and clarity."

- Dorian Van Horn

"It is a sneaky thing, but the reality is we are all just doing our best, and I think it matters less what you did before, and more what you are doing now. As long as you are accomplishing what you need to do in the here and now, does it really matter what you did before and if that stacks up against someone else? I don't think so. There are people with fantastic credentials who are terrible in their roles, and there are people who have had no previous experience who unexpectedly make an incredible impact. **Just embrace any opportunity to learn, and you might surprise yourself**. The world is full of surprising heroes who rose to the occasion. And no matter what, do not let imposter syndrome allow you to keep your team down, or turn you into a micromanager."

- Alyssa Nayyar

"Imposter syndrome is something I've battled along with many other women, especially when stepping into leadership roles or new challenges. Some strategies that have helped me include:

- **Reassurance to myself** when self-doubt arises that all progress will take place outside of the comfort zone and this is a sign that I'm pushing my boundaries and growing.
- **Self-reflection of your personal brand**: Keeping track of all achievements, positive feedback, and successful projects reminds me of my personal brand.
- **Mentors to the rescue**: I have always sought guidance from women who have experienced it all before me and navigated similar struggles, that reassures me that doubt is normal—and that I am not alone."

- Sweta Patel

"The best way I've dealt with imposter syndrome is by realizing most people have it! Instead of pretending like I need to know it all, I'm conscious to ask more questions and clarify to those around me when I'm presented in a new-to-me or unfamiliar situation that I'm learning a new role and may need things explained in detail. Imposter syndrome tends to go away once I learn what is expected of me and how I can bring value to my team and the organization. This can be expedited through regular touch bases with your manager and through personal and professional goal setting using methods such as SMART – Specific, Measurable, Actionable, Reasonable, and Timely. When you complete a goal and check it off the list, you feel empowered and accomplished. Self-doubt occurs from overthinking. People often don't think about us as much as we think about ourselves; this is the case because they're too busy thinking about themselves too! This helps me realize "Its not that big of a deal" and that I should focus on things I can control with positive intent."

- Olga Kocharyan

"I had an extremely tough time dealing with imposter syndrome throughout my career, in various stages, and it still sometimes tries to creep in. I hope that by sharing my story, your strength to believe in yourself shines through and pushes those feelings of doubt away.

To understand why I felt like I didn't belong among my peers at certain points of my career, we need to travel back in time when a naïve twenty-three-year-old woman was desperately trying to become a cop in New Jersey. Not just any cop, a well-paid cop in a very safe city where I had to do little to no work. Remember, I was naïve. I was taking multiple tests and working my way through the system when a family friend recommended a Corporate Security job at a major transportation company. I never turned down an opportunity to interview (neither should you) so I went in, answered some questions, and didn't get an offer. I also did little to no research on what the position entailed, so, in hindsight, I deserved not to get it. I received a call a few days later from the hiring manager offering me another interview for a similar position in Washington, D.C. and again, not turning down an opportunity, took a shot. This time, I managed to secure a Field Physical Security Officer position. It was awesome. I was going to get paid to do Corporate Security. Now I just needed to figure out what Corporate Security was. I had never heard that phrase let alone imagined it as a description of a career. I recall my first week, walking around with a man who was as old as my father, explaining how simplex locks work, still watches, magnetometers, and how to operate a CCTV system. It was the first time I felt completely fraudulent. Not only was I the only woman- that was the least of my issues- I was the only one under the age of forty. I had no idea what I was doing, no clue what I was supposed to do if something happened, and no hint of how anyone could trust me to handle adult things. The next week, I was alone, working midnight until 8 a.m., responsible for the security of approximately 600 employees and oversight of twenty-two vendor guards. I was completely winging it- silently hoping that no major catastrophe occurred that would require me to take any significant action.

It worked, though. Through those eight months, even though I felt like I was a fraud, my work was demonstrating something completely different. My performance reviews were excellent, and eventually, I was recommended for a lateral position, which strengthened my development as an employee.

> **An effective strategy I found successful for me during the early period of my career to combat the feelings of self-doubt was to celebrate my accomplishments, no matter how big or small.**

I kept a notebook of the events that took place, how I handled them, what I did correctly, and areas for improvement. Constant shifting of focus away from self-doubt led me to self-confidence.

As I grew into my career, I realized that building a supportive network of peers who understand the unique challenges faced by women in the physical security field really becomes helpful. Sharing experiences and coping strategies with others who are going through similar struggles can create a sense of community and reduce feelings of isolation. Participating in professional organizations or forums dedicated to women in security can also be a great way to connect with like-minded individuals and gain access to resources designed to empower and uplift. Those organizations came to me much later than I would have liked, so I would recommend building your network as soon as possible.

I first began to join security organizations when I entered management, representing my company. At first, I was so excited to begin speaking to fellow security geeks about investigation techniques, war stories, how they position their cameras, and which risk monitoring tool is the most effective for their team. I figured participation among security organizations would close those gaps that I felt day-to-day, but I was wrong. I quickly learnt that there is a hierarchy among some in security based on public sector careers before switching to the private sector. I was relatively young entering management, and I was a direct hire from college, so I felt that peers often overlooked me because I did not come from a three-letter organization or the military. During some conversations, I began to doubt if I deserved to be in my position and if I was as smart or as capable as the individuals who appeared to have these prominent careers holding similar positions to mine.

To overcome this, I just had to not care about how disrespectfully others treated me and realized that I needed to accept their ignorance. Realize that working for a large company, a small company, public, private, all of it doesn't make one better or more capable. Everyone has great ideas, and the more open you are to listening, networking, and not judging, the more success you will have. I didn't have this breakthrough on my own. I curated a wonderful support system to include multiple mentors and peers who supported and encouraged one another. They worked through my feelings of inadequacy and treatment by individuals who judged me and provided me with reassurance and confidence that I needed.

At the end, **it's crucial to practice self-compassion**. Recognize that everyone, regardless of gender or field, experiences self-doubt at times. Always take a step back and remember what you have done and where you have been, regardless of how long it took or how big or small it was. Each win is a win, and you need to learn to take a moment to celebrate that."

– *Jaime Phair*

"Women in security often feel the challenge of balancing between being tough enough to command respect, but also soft enough to avoid being labeled too aggressive. This balancing act often comes with increased scrutiny, with all eyes either being on you alone, or individual work being credited to a broader team. I vividly remember a day not too long ago where I was the only woman in the room with a group of male colleagues and representatives from the local Federal Bureau of Investigations (FBI) field office. Team leaders had come together to highlight work done by Corporate Security and provide an overview of various teams, programs, and initiatives. While I knew all internal representatives, and several of the FBI partners, being the only women in the room left me with a feeling of inferiority. But why?

The weight of being the only woman in the room adds a level of psychological pressure, the feeling that you alone in that moment are responsible for signifying the importance of a woman's role at the table. While certainly, the entire weight of women's representation was not on my shoulders that morning, it felt as if a place at the security table was. With that feeling in mind, I thought briefly of a saying by Benjamin Lundquist, "Walk into that room as if God himself sent you there." This served as a reminder that when you're the only woman in the room, you own your presence with confidence. That's precisely what I did.

Walking into a room is one thing, but the challenge of managing high-stress environments and situations is completely different. In security, we are often faced with holding the lives of those around us in our hands. Whether your role is operational, intelligence, response, or preparedness, there are outcomes as a result of decisions made, information shared, and actions taken. This can be a heavy burden to bear as women are often hypercritical of every decision we make in a field where second-guessing and wrong decisions can be devastating.

I remember working my first kidnap-for-ransom (KFR) incident involving an employee at my company. As the organization's KFR subject matter expert and program manager, it's my job not only to oversee incident tracking and training, but also to manage incidents when they occur. Several months before this, I remember having a conversation with my manager at the time, expressing my own feelings of inadequacy in taking on such an important role. In that moment, he reminded me of all the training, the knowledge, the contacts I had, and the time I had dedicated to the program, and that regardless of how I felt, he and the entire organization viewed me as a subject matter expert on kidnapping. When the day came, that conversation was the first thing that came to my mind. There was no time to second-guess, there was no time to question my capabilities and knowledge, there was only time to react."

- Paige Wanless

We asked: How have you addressed stereotypes and biases?

"Oh, where to begin...stereotyping, tokenism, bias, isolation, credibility, balancing assertiveness with empathy, harassment, and the list goes on. What I will say is that if you are like me, the majority of rooms or spaces you enter, you scope every potential threat and with that vulnerability of those that occupy it. Knowing that no one, if they see you at all, sees you as a threat, and that can be an advantage...don't ever underestimate this."

- Michelle Rowe

"Stereotypes, bias, and microaggressions "work" because they place the receiving party in an uncomfortable situation in which he or she may not feel empowered to speak up. For this reason, sometimes the aggressor may not understand that he or she is participating in this demeaning behavior. **It's important to be brave and address stereotypes, bias, or microaggression as soon as possible.** This can look like tapping on a friend, manager, or HR for support, or depending on your relationship to the person – having a conversation with them directly. By taking the time to explain how the behavior may be hurtful and educating them on the proper responses, a person may be willing to understand and be thankful you took the uncomfortable time to explain and educate them so they can have more positive interactions in the future. If a person is unwilling or combative about admitting stereotyping, bias, or microaggression, it's important to stay firm in what is "right" and address this behavior each time. Do not ignore or pretend it's okay, do not enable. Escalate as high as needed."

— *Olga Kocharyan*

Allison Sands on Reflection and Tolerance:

Most women in the security industry have a story about how someone in our field, a field of people in positions of trust who dedicate their careers to keeping people safe, have made us feel either physically or psychologically *unsafe*. It's something many in our field, not just women, have come to tolerate and expect, and our attempts at self-preservation are actually working against us.

I didn't always see my own behavior as complicit, until one night following a professional tradeshow. I met a new hire from a company where I had several friends and acquaintances. A group of us decided to grab dinner after the sessions wrapped up, a routine part of networking. There was no reason to be on guard. Until a person in our group, that I had just met (let's call him Troy), started making unsettling jokes towards the women in the group. Since we were in his hometown, he bragged about being able to overpower us and knowing "all the good places to hide a body" in what I can only assume was an attempt to be funny.

What's shocking about this story isn't just what he said, it's how we reacted. Which is to say, we didn't. I even laughed at one point, jokingly challenging his ability to catch us. It wasn't until the fourth time, after he described, in detail, how he would murder someone (me specifically, by this point) that I finally asked him to stop. And it took that long for a friend to step in and back me up.

Then it hit me: bad behavior had become so normalized in these settings that even a fiery-tempered Chicagoan who regularly stands up to bullies and advocates for marginalized groups didn't immediately recognize how far over the line he had crossed. I had taken four threats and required someone else's intervention before I stood up for myself. That realization rattled me just as much as his comments did. I left the gathering shaken and embarrassed by what it said about our industry and about me. How had we reached a point where this kind of behavior was tolerated so long as there were cocktails involved and someone tagged "just kidding" onto the end?

The next morning, I learned that Troy had been fired and was already on his way back home. But that night stuck with me. I vowed to draw a clearer, sharper line between what should be ignored and what absolutely should not. Because if I, someone who prides themselves on calling out unacceptable behavior, could hesitate that long, how many others have stayed silent when they shouldn't have?

Here's what I won't let slide: bullying, blatant racism or discrimination, and any form of sexual harassment. I'm not the appointed guardian of workplace ethics, but I do know how difficult it can be to stand up for yourself, even when every part of you wants to. I also recognize that I have privileges and advantages that many others don't. And if I sometimes hesitate to speak up **despite** all those advantages, I can only imagine how hard it is for those who face additional barriers due to race, nationality, gender identity, sexual orientation, disability, or other forms of marginalization.

That's why we cannot place the entire burden of speaking out on those who are most affected. We can't expect the victims of bias and exclusion also to be the sole advocates for change. Quite the opposite - we must learn from our own experiences, leverage our own voices, and use our positions to make space for others. And now that I'm at a stage in my career where I personally experience less blatant disrespect, I've made it clear: I will be someone who does not tolerate it.

Whenever I speak on this topic, I often get the question from male allies: What can we do to help? My answer is always the same - help us de-normalize the jokes, comments, and behaviors that objectify and demean others. It's not just about choosing not to say something inappropriate yourself; it's also about choosing not to laugh when someone else does. It's about stepping in when you witness something that crosses the line. Because so often, when someone speaks up against inappropriate behavior, they are dismissed as being "overly sensitive" or "unable to take a joke." But when more than one person challenges it, it's suddenly harder to ignore.

I'll never forget the night when I learned first-hand the importance of allyship. At a different security conference, at a different industry dinner, a man made a very inappropriate, sexually explicit comment. I immediately told him the comment was unwelcome and inappropriate. I vowed to speak up after all, and here was a perfect opportunity. His response? He laughed and said this is why he never invited women to professional dinners.

At that moment, I realized that me speaking up wasn't enough. What did make a difference was what happened next. The other men at the table, his peers, stepped in and told him his comment was unacceptable. They asked him to leave. They apologized to me afterward, and the next day, they followed up to make sure I was okay. That is what real allyship looks like. Not just treating others with respect but actively working to make the space better for everyone.

I remember exactly who that man was. I know his name and his company, and I will never do business with him. I can't change his mindset, and I can't make him a better person. But I can control who I work with, who I invite into my professional network, and who I endorse, hire, and support. I can also serve as an ally for others and choose not to accept disrespect as the cost of doing business. Many security companies are waking up to the fact that the industry is shifting - kindness, inclusion, and a strong moral compass are indeed competitive advantages. And that, ultimately, is how we can drive real change.

- Allison Sands

"Stereotypes and biases can manifest in subtle ways—being overlooked in meetings, having ideas attributed to male colleagues, or facing assumptions about technical expertise. Some strategies I've used include: Overcommunicating my personal brand, especially in environments where my ideas may be misattributed or interrupted. Calling it out professionally, if someone interrupts me or repeats my idea as their own, I address it directly yet diplomatically: "I appreciate that you agree with my point. As I mentioned earlier..." Having supportive colleagues (allies)—both male and female—who amplify my voice and reinforce my expertise makes a significant difference. Quantify your battles. If a microaggression occurs, I decide when to educate and when to disengage. **Not every comment deserves my energy, but systemic issues must be addressed.** By mentoring and supporting other women in security, I help create a workplace culture where biases are challenged."

- Sweta Patel

A Global Perspective from Janina Lincke

While there are many challenges in the world for a woman, this set of musings explores the impact of gender on my experience in the security industry.

The security industry is a traditionally male-dominated industry with a large proportion of the workforce stemming from law enforcement, the armed forces, or government. As a civilian female, the impact of this notably male, ex-armed forces and ex-police security workforce is compounded when traveling across geographies and contending with local attitudes to both women, and women in security. Starting in close protection in South Africa,

I walked through the crucible of a patriarchal fire, where heavily conservative expectations on feminine propriety were rife. How to look, how to act, what to say and when to speak at all became even more important when stepping into a profession where women were not welcome, and their value not understood. One year of painful and exasperating lessons imbued me with an awareness that to become a successful human, **I would first have to master myself.** I embraced the vision and then practice of becoming a resilient human. I realized that to protect others meant showing up for myself first, and that only after I streamlined by own existence, was there space to look out for someone else. I empowered myself by choosing who I wanted to be. Instead of bitterly reacting to the world around me, I strove to live with integrity and empathy while maintaining a thick armor. I slowly learned to set firm boundaries, teach people how to treat me, and built the confidence to back myself. I started to maintain my mental and physical health, and consistently invested into my education and EQ. I chose to surround myself with excellent people and take the advice of those who judged me on my merits instead of that which I couldn't control, like being a woman.

I left South Africa for my first international close protection contract at twenty-seven years old and have not looked back since. I've been to almost every continent, meeting a huge number of diverse security people from very different backgrounds. These people were all mirrors in which I saw two main things: firstly, the allies will always be those who can see the bigger picture and it is these people who I have come to seek out. Secondly, there are those who are held back by prejudice, and these people don't matter, unless you let them. My most faithful friend has been Discernment in this regard, and I'm a much better judge of character than I used to be.

The pandemic shut down international travel four years into my career as an international close protection agent and emergency medic. I was in the UK at the time and needed a remote desk job so I stepped into corporate security by joining a global security operations center and then an intelligence team. Many of the gender-based challenges I encountered in performing physical security became white collar misogyny. Gender-based discrimination was less overt and prevalent than in my previous role, and general office politicking and posturing replaced the sexual harassment and outright exclusion from contracts by "old boys' clubs". I feel lucky to have worked in three large multinationals, to witness firsthand how giant organisations operate. I found the corporate culture to only be as healthy as management's attitude, so I decided to become management. I chose to join an organisation whose leadership and ethos aligned with my own fundamental values, and in this company, I created an environment in which my team felt safe to perform their roles. This doesn't mean there hasn't been conflict or challenge, but it's dealt with in a healthy way. I hope that when my colleagues leave, they'll be pulled to a better position, not pushed out by a toxic workplace.

- *Janina Lincke*

* * *

Working in security, or any male-dominated industry, can be tough. Some days, it's subtle. Other days, it's not. The interruptions, the assumptions, the offhand comments, the quiet rooms where your ideas seem to float by unnoticed until someone else repeats them louder. It can erode your confidence if you let it. Don't.

Your voice matters. Your perspective matters. You belong! Finding a way to speak up with confidence without feeling like you have to change who you are is one of the most powerful tools you can possess.

No one has this completely figured out. However, through experience, shared wisdom, and a bit of trial and error, we can improve at making our voices heard and helping others find theirs, too. We're in this together.

4

Men Can Be Powerful Supporters

Representation matters. So does community. However, creating real change in a male-dominated field like security doesn't fall solely on women; it takes allies, advocates, and sponsors who are willing to use their influence to help shift the landscape. These terms, ally, advocate, and sponsor, get used interchangeably, but they each play a unique role:

- Allies show up. They listen, learn, and speak up when it counts, especially in rooms we may not be in.
- Advocates publicly back us. They recommend us for opportunities, challenge bias, and help clear obstacles.
- Sponsors go a step further. They actively put their own credibility on the line to open doors, make connections, and help advance careers.

Given the world we live in, men are often the most connected. They often sit in the spaces where decisions are made and where culture is shaped. When they use that position to challenge bias, promote fairness, and amplify women's voices, it creates real, lasting change. The *vocal lanterns* in this chapter come from individuals who have personally lit our ways as allies, advocates, and sponsors.

Why is Allyship Important?

> Allyship: the state or condition of being an ally: supportive association with another person or group; *specifically*: such association with the members of a marginalized or mistreated group to which one does not belong.[17]

"Allyship in the security industry goes beyond a moral imperative—it's a strategic necessity. When I look at the caliber of women who've taken on top security roles, one thing is clear: a diverse range of perspectives is critical to solving complex, evolving threats. **As I progressed in my career, I noticed our industry often defaulted to the belief that only former law enforcement or federal agents were "qualified" to be security leaders.** Yet in most corporate security roles, we're not tasked with making arrests. Instead, we need professionals who can assess risk, communicate effectively with stakeholders, become viewed as business enablers to our clients and leverage technology in new ways. Over time, I've seen how opening the door to those with different experiences—different genders, ages, backgrounds, and viewpoints—unlocks truly innovative thinking and dynamic teams. Women bring a variety of approaches that spur industry-wide change, whether it's applying new technology to old problems or fostering more collaborative team cultures. My own career has been shaped by individuals who challenged the status quo, believed in my potential, and advocated for me. That's precisely the spirit of allyship I aim to continue."

- Brian Stephens

"Allyship is often a brave act that requires courage and zeal for the celebrated and/or defended person, issue, or cause. Allyship is important because it is

---

[17] "Allyship," *Merriam-Webster.com Dictionary*, Merriam-Webster, accessed August 30, 2025, https://www.merriam-webster.com/dictionary/allyship.

one of the most equitable ways of amplifying voices, ensuring perspectives are heard, seen, and respected. Almost no cause can be won without allies. **Marginalized communities are often subjugated to the point where they tend to lack resources and reach; this is where the ally can be exceptionally helpful.** The ally can also serve as a bridge between the underrepresented group and the majority population, often serving as an ambassador and translator between all sides. Allies tend to educate while confronting behavior and discrimination. Finally, they often leverage privilege and resources to impact change and progress."

- Scott Jones

"I've learned a long time ago that to live the life I want requires being a good person and surrounding myself with other good people. This means being willing to help anyone brave enough to ask for assistance. I think this is essential. **If someone believes I have knowledge or experience that can help them grow in their career, I will help them. Zero hesitation.**

Allyship can take many forms, from having a 1:1 conversation with a colleague seeking advice on advancing their career, to supporting organizations like Women in Security or Global Security Pride. When I am fortunate enough to be asked to participate in forums, I encourage other security professionals to consider building teams that have a myriad of experiences, backgrounds, and approaches. With this diversity, teams can tackle challenges creatively, support one another, and build on one another's strengths."

- Corey Vitello

"It meant and still means being a mentor and helping to open doors and clear obstacles (intentionally or unintentionally) placed in a female security leader's path to success. It could be simple, like creating a mentoring relationship or making a valuable introduction. At times it's more difficult and the discussion can center around experiential gaps or leadership blind spots that need to be addressed before their full potential can be realized."

- Dave Komendat

How can others effectively use their position to support women and other underrepresented groups?

"In our industry, too often women are underrepresented in leadership positions. I don't necessarily believe this is intentional. Law enforcement is generally a male-dominated field, and many organizations draw talent from former police and government agencies. Fortunately, this practice is changing. If CSO's [Chief Security Officers] and people managers truly want professionals who understand the expectations, tempo, and risk-tolerance of corporate organizations (and NGOs, or Non-Government Organizations), they might consider prioritizing candidates with diverse private sector experience. One of the best intelligence managers I've ever worked with had only private sector experience. She was able to navigate the high-pressure demands of the tech sector while never doubting her ability to adapt to the ever-changing corporate risk landscape (not to mention the shifts in fiscal strategies).

Additionally, by volunteering as mentors, we can connect rising stars to our network of industry leaders, heralding their skills and accomplishments. We can answer questions and, if asked, help with organizational and/or professional challenges. We can take an authentic interest in the development and promotion of underrepresented personnel who hold unique perspectives, ideas, and voices, all while upholding a high standard of effort and excellence. We just need to stop talking about doing it and simply do it."

– *Corey Vitello*

Scott Jones on Purposeful and Mindful Actions:

> Purposeful and mindful action(s) can directly impact equity and directed support for women and other underrepresented groups. Advocacy can occur in many forms, including verbal and nonverbal action. Several ways in which this can occur:

Role Modeling:

Raised Voices: Amplifying causes with a focus on any underrepresented group can send a message of acceptance and/or intolerance, particularly from a leadership position. An example of this would be to create spaces where inclusive meetings are the norm. Inclusive meeting: setting the calls, the table, and other environmental factors so that everyone has an opportunity to speak.

Nonverbal Action: Nonverbal, administrative, and the written word can often serve to be more powerful ways of supporting women and underrepresented groups. Not only does the writing become a memorialized artifact of record, the messaging can send a message globally to teams and those that may wish to detract from this type of inclusion. An example of this is to allow for pronouns to be included in: internal company profile pages, signature blocks, and even within virtual meetings.

Process and Policy Modifications/Enhancements:

Inclusive Hiring: Removing bias upstream in the hiring process can be an excellent way of promoting fair and equitable hiring. There has been significant progress in this area over the last decade, particularly amongst tech firms, with some actually removing names on resumes and allowing for fields where candidates can self-identify their pronouns. An example of change: Google has an approach where every new candidate is referred to as 'they' during the process (yes, no 'he/she' is used at all).

Support Equity: Focus on workplace policies that empower employees to present their personal best. This may add flexibility in work schedules (directly supporting parents) through the promotion of pay equity and transparency (many firms are including this as part of their statements and public-facing persona)

Education:

> **Empower People to Learn More:** Leveraging your position to support women and underrepresented groups may be as simple as proving access to corporate, or other, resources. More exists now than ever before and most organizations have significantly invested in materials, training, and access points to support equitable advancement.
>
> - Scott Jones

"If there's one area where every security professional can make a difference, it's in challenging assumptions—both their own and those embedded within their organizations. **By actively endorsing people who don't fit the traditional security mold, you tap into a wellspring of fresh perspectives, insights, and abilities.** This kind of endorsement often flourishes when leaders offer public support, such as recommending up-and-coming talent for key projects, nominating them for awards, or simply highlighting their achievements during team meetings.

Equally important is providing tangible sponsorship, which goes a step further than mentorship by using your own professional capital to open doors. Sponsorship might mean introducing someone to influential decision-makers or vocally backing them during promotion discussions. In tandem, fostering an environment of true inclusion ensures that once people step through those doors, they're set up to succeed. This includes everything from crediting individuals for their ideas in meetings to instituting fair and transparent evaluation criteria for raises and promotions. Finally, never underestimate the power of celebrating the innovation that women and other underrepresented groups bring to the field. Acknowledging and applauding fresh ideas not only builds confidence for those individuals but also signals to the broader security community that diversity is a powerful asset. By taking these steps—big or small—we collectively strengthen the resilience of our teams and shape an industry culture that champions innovation and inclusivity.

Allyship goes beyond simply nodding agreement; it's about challenging traditional notions of who "belongs" in security and opening the profession to a wider range of talents. By recognizing that innovation often comes from those who question norms—often women and other underrepresented groups—you not only lift up individuals, you strengthen the entire industry's resilience. **My hope is that by actively championing and sponsoring these emerging voices, we'll continue to see them lead and inspire, reinforcing that security is far more than an extension of law enforcement; it's a dynamic, evolving discipline that thrives on diversity in every sense.**

I'm grateful to contribute these thoughts, and if a single person reads this and is moved to speak up for a colleague—particularly one who might not fit the traditional mold—then we're making a difference. Together, we can ensure the path forward is one where every talented individual can rise to the top, just as I've seen countless women do, bringing new energy and transformative ideas to the world of security."

- Brian Stephens

Dave Komendat on Inspiration and Intention:

During my 36-year career within the corporate security profession, I had the benefit of working for and alongside some exceptional leaders. Many would say "well, over the course of almost four decades, you absolutely should have been exposed to some great leaders." While I don't disagree with that statement, **what made my experience unique is that several of the most impactful leaders I was exposed to were women, and that is unique because for many years, there were not many women that held leadership roles, especially senior leadership positions within the public or private sector security infrastructure.**

I began my security career at Douglas Aircraft Company as a college intern and I was assigned to my first leader who happened to be a female. Her career journey up to that point was challenging because she did not have the "traditional" background and experience that many of her male colleagues within the security team possessed.

With frequency, both publicly and privately in the workplace she was "reminded " that her background was different, and for many years, not appreciated.

This leader played a key role in my personal development for my entire career. For family and personal health reasons, she intentionally passed on accepting several promotions over the years that would have elevated her to an executive level. Instead, she chose to coach and mentor young talent within our team and help her peers be better leaders, including people like me who were now senior to her.

Because of our long tenure as colleagues, **she would always tell me what "I needed" to hear verses "what I wanted" to hear.** Her perspective and insights were always valued by me and her peer leaders because she was one of the most knowledgeable and tenured managers within our entire leadership team. She was a servant leader who would never take credit for any of the great things she personally accomplished.

Over my executive career, I came to rely on this manager as source of "ground truth and honesty." Her story was one of "choice" where she made an intentional personal decision, (even though she was by far the most qualified candidate most times) to not pursue promotions.

Many other women within the security profession have not made that same intentional decision to limit their career growth within the security profession. Unfortunately, at times within certain environments, the decision to limit their career trajectory has been made "for" them based on internal organizational culture issues.

Based on my long experience with the leader described above (and with other very talented female leaders and high-performing individual contributors), I made the decision to become an active ally for women pursuing leadership roles within the security field.

- Dave Komendat

* * *

Men's support in the security industry, within organizations, and as advocates is priceless as we work toward gender parity. The stories the leaders in this chapter shared show that this doesn't just benefit us; it improves how we protect those we serve in the world. Of course, the bonds we create with fellow women and the communities we build to uplift underrepresented sectors and the performance of the security industry as a whole can help support our journey by tapping into the empathetic nature of those who have traveled the path before us.

5

The Power of Mentorship and Sisterhood

No one makes it alone. Especially not in a field like security. Behind every breakthrough, every new opportunity, every learning moment, there's almost always someone who helped open the door. A mentor. A champion. A friend. Another person who's been where you are, who gets it, and who reminds you that you belong here.

Mentorship and sisterhood are pivotal to how we grow, how we stay resilient, and how we change the face of this field for the next generation. It's about lifting as we climb, sharing hard-earned lessons, creating space for honest conversations, and bringing others along with us.

In this chapter, we'll talk about the real, lasting impact of having (and being) a mentor. The *vocal lanterns* are from women who've made a difference and offer practical tips for building those relationships, as well as a reminder that when we support each other, we all rise.

We asked: What has mentorship meant to you?

"My professional path shifted when **I met the mentor who would change my life**. In my second year of graduate school, a retired four-star general arrived at the University of Texas in the Tom Slick Chair for Peace, an endowed role in my graduate program. He advertised vacancies for research assistants on a topic related to U.S. security roles in Latin America, and I was hired. I found that my stereotypes of military officials and the role of the U.S. military in foreign countries was slowly chipped away as I worked with a kind, brilliant man on the study of policy formation and implementation. To say we were an odd pair is an understatement, with my graduate school flip flops and his daily military regimen. He invested his time and effort in me, taught me about additional nuances and intricacies of foreign and defense policy, and a lifelong friendship formed. He also had the kindness and grace to ask me what my career goals were and said that he wasn't a good supervisor and mentor if he wasn't helping me find a job in my chosen field. In the span of my twenty-five-year career, **he became directly responsible for the three foundational job roles that led me where I am today**. The irony here is that my most influential mentor was not a woman, nor someone who I'd historically thought could be a sponsor and an ally. However, this became the first lesson in mentorship I return to over time: **don't rely on absolutes, never say never, and say yes to opportunities even if they seem unlikely and veer from your intended career path**. If I hadn't embraced the support and guidance offered to me twenty-five years ago, I would not be in a career or role that fulfills me personally and professionally. I'm lucky to say that I have not once regretted my chosen career, largely due to excellent mentorship. Support might come from unexpected sources – don't turn it down just because it isn't in the form you expected."

- Claire Campbell

"There's a quote that I love that goes something like, "Surround yourself with women who would mention your name in a room full of opportunities." Janet is the embodiment of that quote. **She not only opened doors but brought me to the table**. Today, I not only consider her a mentor, but also a friend and my greatest hope is to pay her generosity forward. **I want to be that person who brings others to the table, who helps them find their own path, and who stands beside them as they take a leap of faith**."

- Tristin Vaccaro

"Mentors and sponsors were critical. I work hard. I have always worked hard, and I've earned every good thing that has come to me; but there have been folks along the way who have gone out of their way to shine a spotlight on my contributions, value and potential that inevitably opened doors for me that accelerated my career progress. Folks who gave me opportunities that seemed beyond my level; folks who stood up for me and my work when others questioned it; and folks who gave me the hard yet necessary feedback that made me a better leader. **Find the folks who SEE you, and hold onto them; and then turn around and actively shine a light on others. Don't just open doors; reach back and pull others through**."

– *Jessica Martinez*

Mentorship is an important aspect of growth in any industry, but even more critical in professions where women are underrepresented, like security. So, we asked: How do you find a mentor?

> Industry networks provide exposure to resources beyond an individual's organization. They offer access to a large population of respected, seasoned professionals who can fill the sponsorship role. For security professionals, organizations such as ASIS International[18] (American Society for Industrial Security) and SIA[19] (Security Industry Association) provide both educational and networking opportunities. Within these organizations, there are subgroups specifically designed to support women. These organizations offer education, skill development, and networking that can open doors of opportunity.

"In some cases, mentor relationships evolve naturally among friends or colleagues, and managers and their team members. In other cases, they evolve more formally via mentorship matches organized by non-profits such as Girl Security, higher educational institutions, or industry associations such as

---

[19] ASIS International, the leading professional organization for security management professionals worldwide, provides certification, standards, and global networking opportunities for practitioners. Check out asisonline.org for more info.

[19] Security Industry Association (SIA), founded in 1969, is a U.S.-based trade association representing global security solution providers. SIA provides industry research, market insights, standards development, certification programs, advocacy, and professional networking opportunities for security practitioners and organizations. See securityindustry.org for more info.

ASIS[20] or AIRIP[21]. I would also highlight a third option, which is using your networking skills. Reach out to colleagues or use LinkedIn for informational chats or interviews with people in roles you aspire to, or people whose work you admire. You'd be surprised how many of these individuals are willing to have a conversation to provide insight and guidance. Also, **if an industry leader or advisor asks you to stay in touch, or keep them apprised of your development, or says that they'd be available if you'd like to chat again, then DO IT**. So often young professionals believe they're taking our valuable time or bothering us with questions, but we wouldn't offer our time and insight if we didn't truly mean it."

- Claire Campbell

"When I first tried to break into the field, one of the hardest things was figuring out what the security sector encompasses and where I can and want to fit in. I looked for mentorship via coffee chats, alumni connections, and informational interviews – they helped me learn the lingo, understand the industry better, and set me on the right path. As I moved into different roles and gained more experience, I looked for mentors who could guide me on things like leadership styles, building culture, and developing strategy. These relationships have been super valuable in shaping how I approach my work and lead teams. And now, I try to give back by mentoring others. I believe in paying it forward and helping others the way my mentors helped me."

- Melody Wen

---

[20] See note 17. Check out asisonline.org for more info.

[21] AIRIP (Association of International Risk Intelligence Professionals), a 501(c)(6) nonprofit founded in 2015, empowers risk-intelligence practitioners by connecting, developing, and engaging professionals across business, cybersecurity, reputation, physical security, and political risk sectors through training, networking, and professional development. See airip.org for more info.

What makes a mentor/mentee relationship successful?

"I believe there are three keys to being successful in a mentor/mentee relationship. The first is starting the discussion with someone who you want to learn from; that takes some guts, but it's worth it. I've never come across an industry leader or colleague who has said "no" to anyone asking for a tip or coaching. If you're nervous about asking, then start with asking for advice on a particular topic or two. If you both connect, then you can explore a more recurring connection. The second is **having a plan on what you want to achieve. Mentor relationships shouldn't be griping sessions but instead focused on growth edges**. Come with a plan on what you want to achieve whether its strategy development, improving leadership personas, or navigating career pathways. **Figuring out what skills you want to develop helps to identify who you want to work with.** If you are focused on strategy development, then you should be looking for mentors who have developed programs and organizations. If you want career pathway help, look for people who have roles that you are interested in. The third is having a time-bound objective. Mentoring reliability can fade over time because the participants both feel obligated to keep connecting even after they've met the objectives. **Having a time-bound objective enables you to focus your time together on achieving an outcome**. This, of course, doesn't preclude you from a continued connection, but it affords the opportunity for people to commit easier."

- Kirsten Provence

"I believe that successful women's networks in security have to be built on trust and a shared commitment to keeping doors open and building bridges for other women. Another pathway to success is to support and encourage women to find their own version of success—whether it's working in a specific industry, for a particular organization, in a certain location, achieving work-life balance, or attaining a leadership title. Once we recognize and celebrate diverse definitions of success, we can drive meaningful progress in the field.

I strongly believe in the power of check-ins, even if they're brief. They're a great way to reconnect with people and let them know you're available for a chat or a vent session. This industry can sometimes feel isolating, but knowing you have a community of trusted allies can be incredibly empowering."

- Melody Wen

"It should almost be mandatory that any role you go into, and in any male-dominated industry, **you need to build your army of support from outside** your department, from outside your company, and from multiple teams and levels."

- Brittany Galli

* * *

We all benefit from having a community of professional advisors, advocates, and peer networks. But for women, who are underrepresented in the security industry, they are critical to career progression. What Brittany Galli described in her quote above is building a diverse circle of trusted support—mentors, sponsors, and industry peers—each with a unique role in contributing to your professional success. In her article "Your Personal Board of Directors," Melissa Eisler describes this type of network as five to ten individuals who can help you make sound decisions, give you advice and feedback, challenge your assumptions, broaden your professional network, brainstorm and gut check ideas, and generally expand your perspective and thinking.[22]

> **Pro tip**: Building your personal board of directors takes intentionality and effort. Check out these key steps to build a support network[23]:

---

[22] Melissa Eisler, "Your Personal Board of Directors," *Wide Lens Leadership*, posted [specific date if available], accessed August 25, 2025, https://widelensleadership.com/your-personal-board-of-directors/.

[23] "How to Build an Advisory Board," Forbes, December 14, 2022, https://www.forbes.com/councils/forbescoachescouncil/2022/12/14/how-to-build-an-advisory-board/.

1. Define what you want to achieve and think through potential hurdles.
2. Identify the right "spokes" for your circle—experts, leaders, and peers with whom you can form trusted, mutually beneficial relationships.
3. Commit to purposeful check-ins and communication, and show genuine appreciation.

None of us enters our career fully equipped to tackle every challenge. The act of cultivating relationships itself is a critical skill, but it will also open doors to invaluable experiences and growth. Surround yourself with those you admire, those who want to see you succeed—and grow that spirit of support by guiding those coming up behind you. In other words, be a lantern.

6

The Security Life Balance

"An unknown author once wrote, "The balancing act between career and home is not about doing it all; it's about knowing what matters most in each moment." As women, partners, and mothers, our lives are filled with the feeling of forced balance of doing it all; drop-offs, pick-ups, playdates, grocery shopping, meals, pets, schedules, appointments, keeping a clean and loving home, a happy spouse, work, etc. all while trying to find a moment of peace in between a work day, commute, and the sweet five minutes of self-care you allow yourself. While not all of these things are accomplished every day, that does not mean they are not constantly circling through our mental "to-do" list while we try to spend time with those who matter most. Then, while we are wrapped up in the guilt of letting dishes pile up and only getting an hour of time in with our children... the phone dings. Work."

- Paige Wanless

It's easy to feel like you're supposed to do it all. The security industry demands availability, responsiveness, and constant vigilance without missing a beat at home, with family, or for yourself. And when you can't (because no one can), the guilt creeps in.

But here's what we know: you can't pour from an empty cup. Setting boundaries, protecting your time, and taking care of your well-being isn't selfish; it's necessary. It's how we stay effective in this work and how we stay whole as human beings.

The *vocal lanterns* in this chapter are from women who've faced the same struggles: the late-night calls, the impossible juggle, the quiet burnout no one talks about. They share real strategies for setting boundaries in a 24/7 industry, managing competing priorities, letting go of the guilt, and building self-care practices. You can be committed to this work and still be committed to yourself. In fact, you have to be. And you don't have to figure that out on your own.

We asked: Can you share any experiences with parent, partner and/or pet guilt?

"ALL. THE. TIME. I had my son at a very young age and had parent guilt while trying to finish college and get my career started. I had great opportunities but also limited opportunities because I didn't want to be away from my son. I wanted to be an FBI Agent but would have had to move a lot and be away from my son. The 'mom guilt' was real many times when I'd work holidays or had intense cases while my son was little.

> **It was a difficult balance of feeling like I was either missing out personally or professionally because of timing**.

When my son was older, I took a several month detail in Iraq with the FBI, it was the longest and farthest we'd ever been apart. Luckily, I have a great family and good relationship with his dad but it was still feeling like I was a failure as a mom being away from him. Security can be a 24/7 job and there is the continued imbalance of missing family events, birthdays, anniversaries, etc. which are the mental load many of us carry on a daily basis."

— *Kristin Lenardson*

"I experience all of these often. I have two children, a husband, and a Boston Terrier. Time spent with one is a tradeoff with another. In the last year, I've been more aware of how often I experience guilt. It can become a default loop in my mind after nearly any activity – worked too late…guilt. Took a half-day or remote calls without telling anyone to take my son to track meets…guilt. Didn't dress my kids in the fifty things for dress-up week because I'm overwhelmed…guilt. Made Christmas miraculous, but now husband feels lack of attention…guilt. Packing to take my son on a weekend trip to NYC for 1-1 time, and the dog unpacks my luggage in protest…guilt (LOL). **Despite how hard I can be on myself, the reality is that I'm living a full and complex life. I often remind myself that it is enough**. That, I am enough. I'm allowed to be human, to make choices, and to be okay with them at the end of the day. I don't have to be perfect and I honestly don't think there is a perfect. I also work with a therapist regularly to help identify my own internal parts and patterns and work through life's challenges in a healthy and intentional way. I personally struggle to accept when people may be disappointed with me. Sometimes I can overwork to my own personal detriment, because I am afraid that I will disappoint a boss or coworker, or whomever. I think systemically, women are taught to carry the way others feel, judge, or otherwise respond to their actions. I am learning to not carry other's emotions and opinions. For example, when a coworker is passive aggressive because they don't understand my timing on something, I check in with myself. I say to myself "what do I need?" "am I doing my best in this moment?" and some version of "I know me, I know what I need, I am responsible for me." No one knows more about you and what you need and are capable of in any given moment. I'm learning to not let someone's idea of what I should be doing overwrite what I feel in my body and soul that I need in that moment. I often feel guilty when I'm not at my computer, even though I can be more productive away from my desk. Some of my best ideas come while jogging, but I still feel like I'm cheating or being lazy. If you're thinking about your job, you're working, no matter where you are."

- Liz Maloney

"Prior to becoming a partner and mom, so much of my focus and commitment was on my work and career. Once my family grew, that focus and commitment shifted to include my family in many decisions that I had to make regarding work/career. Where I struggled was trying to show up the same way for my work/career as I did before becoming a partner/mom, without sacrificing time away from my family.

> **The various hats I wore were evolving, yet I didn't know how best to navigate those changes without feeling like I was losing a part of myself or the things I felt most familiar with.**

I'm grateful that through coaching, community, and experience I've discovered the importance of setting boundaries for work, to ensure I'm showing up as the best partner/mom I can be. But on the flip side, I've got a great support system at home that empowers me to be a leader, so I can still pursue my passions and commitment to keeping people safe. Both are so equally important, and giving myself grace to discover how to "harmonize" with these is an individual process everyone can benefit from."

- *Julia Sanya*

"The balancing act of always being "on" while trying to focus on raising a family is one that does not come without significant challenges, guilt, and the daily questions of if I am doing enough for both. It's the constant feeling of guilt for not being home more with my daughter, traveling too much, and too much TV time when daycare unexpectedly closes. It's the stress of presenting on an "on-camera" meeting while everyone sees you get applesauce dumped on your head. It's the desire to grow your family, but not knowing how you will manage finding childcare without a waitlist and balancing schedules. It's all of these things while being vigilant to whatever emergency awaits in your other life. In the security world, there is little opportunity to leave work at work; it follows you home, constantly replaying in your mind. Whether you're responding to threats, escalating intelligence, or managing leadership demands, the margin for error is nearly non-existent. This results in a constant state of stress leading to both physical and psychological harm; I know this from personal experience. Several years ago, I was experiencing severe stomach pains, jumping from doctor to doctor to be told I needed exploratory surgery. Clearly wanting a second opinion, I found a provider who started the appointment by just getting to know me as an individual, not just a patient. It was through those conversations that she suggested I take a short assessment, which ultimately led to the conclusion that I was dealing with chronic stress. The constant levels of stress, coupled with my own lack of self-care, were slowly chipping away at my health."

- Paige Wanless

Working in International Settings with Eva Deren

As a woman working in what is still a male-dominated industry, I would say juggling motherhood and having a career is one of the challenges in various parts of the world. Over the years and decades, I have become rather pessimistic when it comes to gender equality. The 'have it all' myth just is not realistic, and as women struggle with how to forge their personal path, the expectations on a woman from not only society's expectations, but also her own personal generations of ancestors and family history, help to shape her way in the world.

A working mother has a hard time competing in the workplace with a peer who has no children or who has a stay-at-home spouse (although I didn't say mom, let's think about what percent of those spouses are moms...), and she will have an impossible time competing in the 'mom space' with a parent (again...mom) who is pretty much devoted to raising children. I have lived in countries where the norm is to have paid help with the children, and this definitely makes it much easier in the workplace. Flexibility regarding working from home helps reduce the pressure especially parents of younger children may feel when it comes to showing up for the kids without having to take PTO (paid time off) every time. In my opinion, the one thing that would contribute to gender equality in the workplace would be for men to be as present as women when it comes to raising their children, each and every day.

- Eva Deren

Then we asked: How do you navigate leading a team, function or process while managing responsibilities outside of work?

"Being in security, sometimes you have to focus on the tactical work instead of the strategic work. In these instances, while trying to manage work responsibilities, sometimes it was day-by-day, when I could only complete the work that was absolutely necessary that day. **I did let personal relationships and friends and family down at times because of work.** I do prioritize workouts and (trying to) eat healthy to combat stress, but these also fall off due to the work load. Sometimes you can only get done what is absolutely needed in one day and know the rest will be there tomorrow, plus more to do."

- Kristin Lenardson

"I've tried everything from strict time-blocking every fifteen minutes to completely winging it. On average, I am well organized and I work hard, but I couldn't manage it all without a couple of key dynamics:

1. **Flexibility**: I work from home, have a lot of flexibility in my schedule, and I am three-hours ahead of my team. When I have personal conflicts in the day, I can (and often do) take meetings from my cell or work late after my kids go to bed.
2. **I have assistance**: I have a house cleaner once a week. My sister picks up my kids at school two days a week, and my husband and I divide the rest. I felt overwhelmed by the prospect of organizing my garage after our recent move, so I hired someone to do it. I have learned to ask for

help, especially after having a second child during COVID. I decided it was sometimes necessary to pay for the assistance I need. You need to adapt as you age, have children, or your work or personal dynamics change."

– Liz Maloney

"It comes down to putting your greatest asset first; people. I do my best to create an environment where I encourage my team to take care of themselves and their families, and support one another, so that when they show up for work they're able to give their best. And if they're unable to give their best at work because of life events, they know that we're there to support them and pick up where they've left off. **The only way I'm able to manage my responsibilities outside of work while also leading others and operations is by emulating this level of care.** I'm able to prioritize my responsibilities outside of work because I have a team that I can depend on and extend the same level of grace and support I provide them. This requires a level of vulnerability, trust, and empowerment that has to be fostered over time."

– Julia Sanya

"It's important to highlight the value of supportive peers and employees on your team who make it possible for you to keep pushing forward when social expectations want to hold you back. **I'll never forget how my employees and peers welcomed my six-month-old daughter in the conference room when a critical conversation needed to happen, and I didn't have childcare.** I'm forever grateful to the folks who respected the blocks in my calendar when I had to pump as a breastfeeding mom, and to the leaders who would move meetings so I could leave early to make my son's soccer game. They did this while still giving me important projects, leadership roles, and promotions. That's the key part - unconditional support. Empowering folks - especially women - to be successful at home without penalizing them at work."

– Jessica Martinez

What boundaries are necessary when work involves constant connectivity?

"The boundaries in the security field are almost nonexistent. Security and safety can be physical, legal or regulatory issues, but it is also a feeling - does someone feel safe and secure. In these instances, you are managing an incident, but often you are also managing how people feel about the incident. In these cases, there is no 'day off' or personal hours. It does take a healthy respect for the position, but also to know if you work 10+ hours one day, you can (maybe) work 6+ hours another day. You can push back a little on time, but this is not a 9-5, Monday through Friday position. **Knowing this, the balance is being available when it is needed and taking some time back when you can. It took me many years to learn this, and unfortunately, I'm still not great at setting boundaries.**"

- Kristin Lenardson

"Do whatever helps you sleep. Silence notifications. Don't respond to messages immediately. Meditation and work that helps you be in the present. Get outside. **Look up to the sky as often as possible.**"

- Liz Maloney

"What I find interesting about boundaries is that many of us set them from the mindset of implementing rules and limits for what others can and can't do to us, but I find that setting boundaries for others isn't as challenging as it is to set boundaries for ourselves, particularly when it comes to work that involves constant connectivity. But **developing boundaries for yourself requires self-awareness**, and work that's necessary, in order to thrive in a role where it involves constant connectivity. It's almost a way for you to protect your own values and priorities from yourself and the habits you have that can lead to violating your values and priorities. When I started to develop boundaries for myself, it required me to get clear on what mattered to me most, and also what

I prioritized in that particular season of my life. It required discovery, patience, trial and error, self-accountability, and not wavering out of guilt, which is something I find many women in particular struggle with, especially earlier on in their careers. Once I discovered what worked for me, I felt empowered and was able to optimize my energy and focus. A few of my necessary boundaries when it comes to work include:

- Prioritizing my family's events and schedule despite what meetings or work events I may miss
- Manage expectations by assessing urgency, delegating work appropriately, and/or negotiating workload to include deadlines based upon personal and/or team's capacity
- Coaching my team through problem solving instead of directly solving the issue in order to empower them, develop them, and capitalize on my time
- Limiting when I check and respond to emails. (i.e. easing into my morning before checking/responding to emails and not responding to emails after hours, unless they're critically urgent.)
- Calendar blocks to recharge and for self-care and taking time off a few times a year (vacations and staycations)
- Implement self-coping practices to remain calm and protect my energy, in order to not absorb other's projected energy (still a work in progress for me)."

- Julia Sanya

What self-care practices are effective in security careers? What strategies help maintain emotional well-being?

"Friends are the best self-care practice. Having individuals who understand what I'm going through because they have also been through it, and can chime in with advice or encouragement is the best. At one position, I learned someone with a mental health disorder had taken their life. I had gone through all the security protocols I knew to do but when I learned about the incident I called a friend in the industry. We both knew there wasn't more I could have done, but it helped just to have someone listen and let me be sad for a bit. Being able to process our emotions in security is not often discussed and the impact of the incidents does take a toll after all these years. I am also a big fan of working out for stress, but everyone needs to do what is best for their minds and bodies; this may be reading, spending time with family, or going for a quick walk."

— Kristin Lenardson

"Therapy, therapy, therapy. I go weekly. Having personal interests and outlets that aren't about your work or your family. Exercise and sun."

— Liz Maloney

"Self-care practices are critical in order to manage stress and improve our overall quality of life in order to overcome the unique challenges we face in security. As security professionals we tend to be inundated with potential threats and risks each day. Over time this can become taxing to our mental health and directly impact how we see the world and interact with others. It's important that we process and work through these mental and emotional stressors. A few ways to do that include therapy, mindfulness/meditation practices, journaling, support groups, etc.

Sleep, eating well, and exercise are self-care staples you will always hear about. But in security, it's critical that we stay alert, have situational awareness, and assess the environments and people we're protecting. In order to do this, we have to be energized, attentive and focused, which requires our minds and bodies to be operating optimally.

Lastly, I would recommend exploring your creativity, learning something new, or connecting with nature. These may sound as simple as hobbies, but these are unique ways to recharge, invest in ourselves, and expand our skillsets. In security we're constantly solving problems which requires us to develop new strategies to mitigate risks and respond to threats. By exploring our creativity, learning, and connecting with nature, we're able to not only care for ourselves, but also bring ingenuity to the work we do."

- Julia Sanya

"Self-care is not an indulgence, it's a necessity. It's preservation. We often think of self-care as inspirational quotes or spa days, but in reality, it is about sustaining your mind and body so that you can fulfill your responsibilities and have a piece of yourself left at the end of the day. So how do we do this? One of my personal favorites is intentional decompression. In the security world, debriefing is standard practice, whether it is after an assessment, an incident, or other critical event, but what is often overlooked is mental decompression. Being intentional in this practice helps the body return to neutral from a state of constant readiness, allowing yourself to create a space between work and real life. For many, this can be journaling, exercise, or music; it can also be taking a moment of stillness, breathing exercises, or truly letting yourself feel what you had numbed yourself to that day. Without this time, layers begin to mold together where we find ourselves between what matters most at different moments.

Therapy and peer support is both a critical and underutilized resource in the security field, especially for women who feel they lack the time or confidence to attend. Therapy can provide a space to process stress and trauma, build emotional resilience, as well as providing opportunities to learn the value of boundaries between your operational identity and personal self. This is particularly important for women who are mothers and partners who need help separating the two identities. Setting healthy boundaries for yourself doesn't have to be overly complex, you can say no to the extra meeting, you can take a personal day, you have permission to ignore a non-critical email until tomorrow morning. Boundaries are recognizing that at the end of the day, you cannot give to others if you, yourself, are running on empty. We, as women, need to be reminded of that more."

— Paige Wanless

Andreea Patra on Her Quest for Balance:

At Bank of America, I have been fortunate to hold many roles, first as an analyst, then team manager, and ultimately, director, and while my roles have changed, one thing has been consistent: the struggle to balance working and family. At first, I did not realize that these two aspects of my life were so out of balance...but I learned that if you look closely, the signs are all around you. For me, little glimpses came through when my daughter would not know her ABCs but she knew the name of my manager or when she did not know the difference between a city and a state but she knew there were these people out there called "protesters." Ouch, right?! It was glaringly obvious when my older son would walk over when I worked late nights and try to close down my laptop screen...the signs were all around, I just needed to stop for a minute and see them.

I like to think that as I got older, I grew wiser when it comes to work-life integration (not sure one ever gets to permanent "balance," so do not feel guilty if you feel like you cannot get it quite right some days). I learned that I needed to be clear and vocal about how I needed to spend my time, both with my boss and with my family. This means that while some days I might need to be online at odd hours, I try to make up that missed family time in days when work does not require me to be connected. Notice I said "require" as sometimes, so many of us in this line of work are so driven by a sense of service, duty, and passion that we feel like/want to be connected or send that one extra email (which could really wait until morning). So, one piece of advice: be really honest with yourself about when you are required to work.

The hardest part in this quest for work - life integration for me (and many other amazing women I have met along the way) - is taking time to focus on myself. There is always another report, another email to respond to, another after-school activity to drive the kids to or another pile of laundry haunting me in the corner, and it can feel so wrong to focus on me with all that swirling around. While I still falter some days, I do now understand that pursuing my passions (be it travel or volunteering) helps me be a more energized, compassionate and calm leader and mom/wife: so simple yet so true, that one cannot give from an empty cup.

So, whether you are just starting on this security journey or you are years into it and, like so many of us, still on the quest for work-life "balance," I hope you know that it starts with you. **It starts with you being honest and compassionate with yourself and being vocal about some simple boundaries** (tip: start small, one micro-step at a time, like "for the next two hours, I am not checking emails"). Remember that you owe yourself some me-time, and will be better for it and just as important, remember that you are NOT alone in this journey! Find someone you can commiserate with, and who will remind you (and likely, while doing so, remind herself) that you are doing your best and that's enough most days! We are here with you and here for you!

- Andreea Patra

What's the secret to thriving?

"In order to thrive in a role, I have found there are three key things you must have — a supportive manager, work that is interesting, and opportunities for growth. What that looks like is different for everyone, I'm not a fan of prescriptive rules on this and it will change as your career evolves. Early on it may look like promotional opportunities, later on, it may mean the opportunity to push yourself in other ways. I think it is also important to keep in mind that every job is going to have bad days, or even weeks or months, just as life does. There also may be times where a good manager and interesting work are enough. However, if you reach a point where you no longer have any of those three things, I personally think it is time to move on. There are also outside factors that I think we tend to forget. All of my work moves were driven by running toward something, rather than away from something else!

The most important thing to remember is that **you are the only one who has the full picture of your life, your goals, and your ambitions and knows what is right for you**. I have found that the times I went wrong in my career were the times I let someone else coach me too much into doing something that wasn't genuine or real for me - staying true to myself, has been the most critical factor that has allowed me to thrive in the workplace."

- Alyssa Nayyar

"Thriving in the workplace begins with understanding that you deserve a seat at the table. You're here because you deserve to be here! Isaac Newton was just sitting under an apple tree one day and discovered the force that keeps us all quite literally grounded. Once you realize that people are interested in your thoughts and the value that you add to the every day, you become energized to share, ask questions, contribute, and end your day feeling accomplished – thus allowing yourself to rest and restore.

Thriving begins with finding passion in your work. There are a million jobs out there, how do you know this is the right one for you? How do your values align to your day-to-day output? **I always knew I wanted to protect people**. I had several potential thoughts for careers paths prior to landing on physical security and cybersecurity, but they always centered around protecting people: criminal defense attorney, corrections officer, mental health counselor. In the end, I chose a profession where each day I know that I'm making a difference in the lives of people – sometimes in ways that they will never be able to physically touch or see but I know it's happening, and that's enough.

Thriving also looks like looking for, and leaping towards, that next challenge. There is something to be said about being nervous and doing it anyway. Once you know that you can overcome that hurdle, the next one seems more doable. You gain new skills and experience that translate to more new hurdles, more new leaps, and more confidence.

But for me, it's also remembering that I'm so much more than just my job. You are so much more than just your job. Work is one important part of your life that fits into the puzzle of your entire image. If tomorrow work leaves, you are a friend, daughter, sister, partner, aunt, you are the books you read, the food you eat, the laughs you share, the memories you make, the tears you cry, you are you."

- Olga Kocharayan

How do you know when it is time to walk away vs. stick it out?

"At some point in our careers, we go through moments when you have to decide whether to persevere in a challenging environment or move on. Some guiding questions I ask myself:

- **Am I respected?** Respect is the fundamental requirement for me to attach my personal brand with any mission. Am I respected genuinely or am I being the victim of the passive aggressive nature of work environment. It is difficult to measure; however, how you are treated while having tough professional conversations or navigating a tough decision-making situation can be good foundations to validate how you were treated.
- **Is the challenge temporary or systemic?** If a company has a toxic culture with no signs of improvement, it may not be worth staying. If the company culture is supportive but there are challenges with my specific work-environment, if my contributions are overlooked despite efforts to advocate for myself, it may signal that it's time to seek a more supportive environment.
- **Am I growing?** If I am still learning and expanding my skills, it may be worth working through challenges.
- **Does this align with my long-term goals?** Sometimes, a short-term struggle leads to long-term career growth, but if a role no longer aligns

with my aspirations, I explore other opportunities."

- *Sweta Patel*

"There will always be periods of hardship in all life events. For me, **I know it's time to walk away from a situation when I can no longer learn and grow from the situation.** Growing pains are true, they can be uncomfortable. But if it is just pain and I am no longer being supported physically, mentally, and emotionally with no output — it's just a waste of time and life."

- *Olga Kocharyan*

"Knowing your worth is fundamentally critical to owning your own career development and advancement. Reflecting on my journey, I wasn't worth much when I first started out, because I simply didn't know anything. My education and certifications weren't a substitute for real world experience, so my compensation as an entry-level US government analyst reflected that. During my first decade on the job, I took on every challenge that I could find and worked hard to gain experience and expertise. I earned recognition and awards while I took on greater responsibilities, but I also hit a ceiling on promotion. I spent over eight years at the same pay grade and was continuously told I wasn't eligible to apply for the next level role. It took me too long to realize that not only was I undervalued, I was never going to be promoted. When I finally acknowledged it, it was easy to leave. I was offered a seat on the rocket ship called Facebook and I never looked back."

- *Suzanna Morrow*

* * *

We began this chapter with Paige Wanless' words, and it is fitting to end with hers as well:

"Being a woman in security while integrating a life at home is to move through a world not built for you. It is to carry grit and gentleness in the same breath, make decisions that impact lives in the morning to come home to children and a partner who need you in the evening. It is to walk into a room, standing alone as a woman, but stand out in your ability to lead. At the end of the day, it is not about finding balance, balance will never truly exist. It's learning to integrate two opposite worlds on your own terms, without apology, and truly understanding what matters most, when it means the most."

- Paige Wanless

III

Taking It to the Next Level

7

Security Entrepreneurship

For some, success in security means climbing the ladder. For others, it means building the ladder from scratch. Security entrepreneurship isn't for the faint of heart. It takes vision, resilience, and more than a little courage to start your business, launch a consultancy, develop new solutions, or create something entirely your own. For the women who've done it, it's also one of the most rewarding, empowering ways to make an impact. It's a way to shape the work, the culture, and the future of security on your own terms.

The *vocal lanterns* in this chapter are from women who've taken that leap. Whether you're dreaming of launching your own security business or just curious about what it takes, their experiences will remind you that you don't have to follow the path, but sometimes, you get to build it.

Let's talk about what it means to bet on yourself and how women are reshaping the security industry, one bold idea at a time.

* * *

Kathy Lavinder Bets on Herself:

Becoming an entrepreneur is betting on yourself. I have to admit it was an easy choice for me because I have not experienced imposter syndrome. With a lot of family support and encouragement in my childhood, I was lucky to always have the self-confidence to jump into the new and the unknown. Also, I had the benefit of living through first wave feminism, learning from the writings and taking to heart the advice of feminist icons. "I am woman, hear me roar," may sound cringe now, but it was empowering back in the day. I haven't forgotten those early days when I was the only woman in a newsroom or in the management ranks. It was lonely in some ways, but I developed strong working relationships with my male colleagues and I always knew they had my back.

I know that others without the same foundational support I had, or for other reasons, may wrestle with self-doubt and prefer caution. Caution is fine, but don't let self-doubt stop you from maximizing your potential. My advice is to take baby steps, as confidence can be developed over time. Small successes will reinforce your belief in you. Remember that you are your harshest critic and you should give yourself grace, as easily as you do to others.

I have to say, upon reflection, that the security arena, being so male dominated, was a tough one to break into. **I just kept banging on the doors, and when given any opening, barged in.** I found allies along the way and am grateful for their support to this day. To any budding entrepreneur, my advice is to identify and then cultivate your allies, your brain trust, and your targets of opportunity. The security sector is exceptionally robust with lots of growth potential if you have an idea, a solution, a plan, and the drive to make a difference.

Develop relationships and partnerships with other sector aligned entrepreneurs, since you can be stronger and more successful together. Be the face of your organization and your brand in the marketplace so that when people have a need you're top of mind. Take business courses or read books about business to become well versed in the core competencies needed to run a successful business. Identify your weaknesses and hire others, when possible, to bring those strengths to your business. Be realistic and patient as you grow your business. Always be grateful for those who put their trust in you and your enterprise.

- *Kathy Lavinder*

We asked: What forged your path to entrepreneurship?

"Building intelligence programs in the private sector was such a new field then that I got involved with counterparts at other oil and gas companies – and eventually other multi-nationals – and we all figured out how to do this together, as we soon realized how different this was to intelligence work in the US government. I spent several years there – learning about business, about how it intersects with global security and about entrepreneurship – particularly when I was recruited to work at a much smaller company. I left that company in 2014 as a result of a downsizing and decided to try something different. I had no idea at the time that my consulting would turn into a full-blown multinational company, but it has been so interesting and so much fun to build. I wouldn't have it any other way."

- *Meredith Wilson*

"After more than fifteen years in security and another five in technology and gaming, I found a new purpose: creating workplaces where people could thrive—both personally and professionally—at every level and in every industry. I had seen firsthand how unnecessarily difficult many organizations make it for people to do their best work in healthy, sustainable ways—not just in security but across all fields. My experience in security taught me how deeply ingrained industry cultures shape workplace dynamics, for better or worse. That realization fueled my drive to build something different."

- *Jessica Martinez*

Tristin Vaccaro on Inspo Through Mentorship:

Never in a million years did I think I would be a full-time freelance content writer in the security industry. I never majored in writing or journalism, and I certainly never considered a career in security. But through extremely lucky circumstances, some hard work, and support from incredible mentors, colleagues, and friends, I've ended up exactly where I'm meant to be.

I was introduced to the security industry in 2021, after spending four years in the same inside sales role in the tradeshow industry. A former colleague had transitioned to an access control company that was hiring for a sales account executive role. It felt like the right opportunity, so I took the leap. But as I settled in, I realized the problem wasn't the industry- it was the fit.

Sales was never a place I saw myself long-term. After majoring in public relations in 2017, I took the first job offered to me – the inside sales job. I had dreamed of working in non-profit PR or marketing, but I prioritized stability over passion. In this role, I would find ways to showcase my creativity by organizing events and managing social media strategy. But this came at a cost. Late nights in the office and constant burnout became the norm. I was giving more than I received, and I began questioning whether this was the place for me.

By the time the COVID-19 pandemic hit, I knew I had to leave. I wanted something that would reignite my passion, and when the sales opportunity at the access control company came up, I hoped it would be the change I needed. But after a few months, I realized that once again, I was being drawn to the creative side of things. I felt most fulfilled when writing client case studies or refreshing brochures, but it still wasn't enough.

A few months into this new role, an opportunity arose that would change everything. The company encouraged industry newcomers to apply as mentees to the Talent, Inclusion, Mentorship, and Education (TIME) program. The TIME program, organized by the Security Industry Association and its RISE Committee, matches mentees with experienced professionals in the security industry who provide guidance and support. I had never heard of SIA or RISE, SIA's young professionals' community, but I applied nonetheless.

This is where luck played a pivotal role in my entrepreneurial journey—luck and the incredible intuition of Katie Greatti, the SIA representative who matched me with my mentor, Janet Fenner. I remember reading Janet's profile among the mentors and thinking she was exactly who I wanted to be like when I "grew up." She owned her own marketing agency and seemed passionate about creating for the benefit of the security industry. I recall marking her down as my top choice on my mentee application.

One of the first things Janet asked me on our first call was what I did. I remember telling her verbatim, "I'm in sales, but I've always wanted to work in marketing." Any other mentor would have said, "That's nice." She took this as a call to action.

She started asking me what aspects of marketing I enjoyed, what my goals were, and what I wanted from a marketing career. I think she picked up on my passion for storytelling before I could even express it. She also knew that the industry needed skilled writers. It wasn't long before I considered leaving my full-time role to pursue freelance content writing.

I could say that Janet gave me all the encouragement I needed to make it happen. But she did so much more than that. She brought me along with her to my first security technology conference and trade show. She introduced me to people who would eventually become my first clients. And she gave me a front-row seat to see what a female powerhouse in the security industry looked like. Watching her in action, leading conversations, building relationships, and shaping the narratives of some of the biggest brands in security changed the entire trajectory of my career.

When we returned, I quit my full-time sales role to start freelance content writing. It was terrifying, but less so knowing that I had Janet's full support. I knew she wouldn't let me fail, but more than that, I knew I wouldn't let me fail. For the first time, I wasn't just following the career path of least resistance. I was building my own.

- Tristin Vaccaro

"During my time in the industry, I noticed a consistent gap in how organizations approached security transformation—many had technical tools and operational skills but lacked strategic alignment and internal capability to lead change with diverse stakeholder groups. That realization shaped an idea for a specialized consulting focus, helping security leaders evolve their programs to strategic functions and show them the best path to execute their vision. The first step I took was doing more of this within my own organization, learning and perfecting my craft, and increasing my experience. I had often considered the leap into entrepreneurship, but I was always too scared to take it.

Then, in the midst of that upward climb, life came to an unexpected and stressful impasse. I was diagnosed with early-stage breast cancer. I was fortunate: after surgery and a month of radiation, I was cancer-free. But the experience left its mark. A diagnosis like that forces a person to reflect—to reevaluate what matters most. For me, it was time to revisit my canvas and begin designing the next chapter.

I believe in having a practice of 'checking in' with oneself—weekly, sometimes daily. For me, it's a journal, music, and a comfortable chair. I write, I reflect, I ask what's working and what's not. It's through this process that I shape my goals and direction.

Leading up to my leap into entrepreneurship, those check-ins revealed consistent themes: a desire to create, to build, to learn, to prove to myself that I could do it, and to shape a life structure aligned with my values. I also saw a real need in the industry for the experience and skills I had cultivated. I found alignment, where my desire met with purpose and a true industry need—and the entrepreneurial path became clear.

Entrepreneurship, at its core, requires courage and self-trust. Security professionals often underestimate the transferability of their skills to entrepreneurship. People often say to me, 'You're so brave'—which I suspect is their polite way of saying, 'You're kind of nuts,' ha! But it's true—**starting a business takes guts and thoughtful planning**. So far, the journey has been filled with adventure, growth, and reward. **It's scary. It's hard. But it feeds every part of me that wanted to build, learn, and stretch beyond the known**.

What I love most is that now, my canvas is always out. I'm constantly designing, evolving, and iterating during this early phase of business-building—and it feels incredibly aligned. While my company is relatively new, we've already had the privilege of helping organizations mature their security processes. The success is real and growing, yet I'm still defining what this chapter will become. And I've come to believe that as an entrepreneur, the 'figuring it out' is never done. Each client, each opportunity, each connection is a new challenge—a new canvas. And that excites me.

I was fortunate to have several mentors and friends—women in their sixties and seventies—who left a lasting impression. What stood out most was how many of them had reinvented themselves, often multiple times, both professionally and personally. Whether navigating career pivots, children, divorce, international moves, or other life changes, they had all crafted rich, beautiful lives that aligned with who they were in each chapter. From them, I learned a powerful truth: I didn't need to know who I wanted to be 'forever,' just how to align my life to my current desired chapter. This made navigating career changes easier, with less pressure to always have the right answer. Since then, I've viewed my career as a canvas—one I can create and recreate endlessly, so long as I'm willing to do the work."

- Liz Rice

What support systems are needed to encourage more women entrepreneurs?

"I think there is a lot of great support out there already that may not be security specific, but that have been designed with entrepreneurs in mind. In the early days, for me, being around other people who were also creating something new was an essential learning experience – and really important for my overall morale. So, I joined a co-work space. There are groups all over the country that support entrepreneurs, including innovation hubs in medium to larger towns across the US that will teach you the basics of entrepreneurship. As your business grows, you'll also find different types of support at different times. Advisors, professors, former bosses, peer business owners and other entrepreneurs all become important as you move from one professional puzzle to the next."

- Meredith Wilson

"**Better access to capital**: Women received just 2% of total VC funding in 2023, and the numbers are even lower in traditionally male-dominated industries like security and tech. This funding gap isn't just about bias against women founders—it's also about the lack of women decision-makers in venture capital. The more we elevate women into leadership roles in both security and VC firms, the more funding will flow to women-led security businesses, giving them the critical early investment they need to succeed.

A cultural shift in caregiving expectations: The reality of "mom guilt" is inescapable, even in supportive, egalitarian partnerships. Societal norms still expect women to bear the brunt of caregiving, making it incredibly difficult to build a business while managing family responsibilities. We need to normalize shared caregiving and 'village' support systems—whether through family, friends, or paid help—so that women entrepreneurs have the time and mental space to grow their businesses without guilt or burnout."

- Jessica Martinez

What professional development resources are most valuable for aspiring women security entrepreneurs?

"I don't think there's a lot formalized around being a female security entrepreneur, but there is a lot out there to support female entrepreneurs in general and security professionals in general. I think the best way to find those resources is to figure out what you need – and then plug into the organization best suited to assist you. There are awesome networks of women and men that are genuinely interested in supporting and learning from one another. It can take a while to find your people, but they are out there. It might be in an academic course, it might be in a group like Chief[24], it might be a friend or mentor – it's probably all of the above. Be flexible and remember that those needs will change depending on what stage of your company's development you are at."

- Meredith Wilson

"Most security professionals have deep expertise—whether in physical security, intelligence analysis, or investigations. Their skills and services are valuable. But many lack the operational knowledge required to run a successful independent firm rather than functioning as an expert within a corporate structure. To bridge this gap:

- **Take an entrepreneurship course**. Understanding business fundamentals—corporate taxes, financial planning, legal structures—will save you from costly missteps.
- **Expand your network**. Talk to founders and startup CEOs who have built businesses from the ground up. Learn from their successes and failures.
- **Prioritize learning outside your comfort zone**. You already know your core skill set. Focus on what you don't know—customer journey mapping,

---

[24] Chief is a private, invitation-only community launched in 2019 for senior women executives, offering peer-group circles, executive coaching, and leadership education. Check out https://chief.com for more info.

content marketing, proposal writing, sales funnels, and tech stacks. These are the skills that will make or break your business.

It's tempting to stay in the familiar territory of your expertise. Don't. Lean into the discomfort. Push through the learning curve. It won't just improve your chances of success; it will refine and elevate the product or service you bring to the world."

- Jessica Martinez

Practical Insights from Liz Rice:

> To those who are thinking about entrepreneurship, I encourage you to think about the fact that first, Entrepreneurship doesn't always mean launching a full-scale company. For some, it's consulting between roles, freelancing, or leading internal innovation. There are many ways to take ownership of your work and build something impactful. To prepare yourself for an entrepreneurial or intrapreneurial background, I strongly recommend investing in your education and certifications and becoming involved in communities that align with your goals.
>
> Stimulating your mind, expanding your network, and learning from people outside your circles are invaluable ways to gain clarity and vision. Your mind is a muscle, and the more you challenge it, the stronger it becomes. There are a few of the most practical insights I can offer to women in the security industry pursuing intrapreneurship or launching their own ventures:

- Check in with yourself often - Log and celebrate your wins
- Learn from your mistakes and from the mistakes of others
- Surround yourself with amazing people - be curious and listen to their stories

- Be brave and believe in yourself – Stay curious and keep your canvas active
- Find the spot where your drive meets a real industry or company need
- Remember: you can create and recreate yourself through every chapter, as long as you're willing to do the work
- Offer to lead or consult on internal projects that cross departments
- Shadow or interview someone running their own security consultancy
- Read up on business basics: proposals, pricing, contracts
- Start building a niche – what problem do you love to solve?

> **Some resources I return to again and again:**
> *Unapologetically Ambitious* by Shellye Archambeau[25]
> *Designing Your Life* by Bill Burnett and Dave Evans[26]
> *The Crossroads of Should and Must* by Elle Luna[27]
>
> – Liz Rice

* * *

As we've explored the remarkable impact of women driving innovation and entrepreneurship in security, it becomes clear that individual vision and leadership ripple outward, shaping the industry as a whole. The next step is to take these lessons and look forward and examine how today's trailblazers and their pioneering ideas are influencing the trajectory of security, and how we can collectively shape a safer, smarter, and more well-lit future.

---

[27] Shellye Archambeau, *Unapologetically Ambitious: Take Risks, Break Barriers, and Create Success on Your Own Terms* (New York: Grand Central Publishing, 2020).

[27] Bill Burnett and Dave Evans, *Designing Your Life: How to Build a Well-Lived, Joyful Life* (New York: Alfred A. Knopf, 2016).

[27] Elle Luna, *The Crossroads of Should and Must: Find and Follow Your Passion* (New York: Workman Publishing, 2015)

8

Shaping the Future of Security

The future of security isn't something we sit back and wait for. It's something we shape with every decision, every conversation, every person we lift along the way. Across the industry, women are stepping up, speaking out, building companies, mentoring the next generation, and reshaping what this work looks like and who it works for. The path hasn't been easy. It still isn't. But the *vocal lanterns* throughout this book have shown that change is already happening in quiet moments of mentorship, in bold career moves, in the voices that refuse to be ignored.

In this final chapter, we look ahead. To the challenges still to be faced. To the opportunities still to be created. And to the role each of us has in building a more inclusive, resilient, and forward-thinking security industry. The future doesn't belong to those waiting for permission. It belongs to those willing to build it... and we're already getting to work. Let's light those lanterns.

> As the former chair of the Global ASIS Women in Security Community, I'm so proud to be part of this security industry, the WIS (Women in Security) communities, and only 13% of the workforce. Data tells a story; this gender gap isn't just a fairness issue—it's a critical barrier to the industry's ability to innovate and compete on a global scale. We only have so much time to make a change exponentially. The

need for women in security is clear, and with the support of hiring managers and leadership finally on our side, it's time to bring in the talent to match the growing desire for change.

I've seen firsthand how our underrepresentation reflects broader gender and pay disparities. But research consistently shows that when women are present and included, companies thrive. McKinsey's 2020[28] report found that companies with more diverse workforces are 36% more likely to experience above-average profitability. In security, the inclusion of women brings fresh perspectives, new ideas, and innovative solutions. With the industry facing increasingly complex and evolving threats, diverse teams are better equipped to develop creative solutions and address challenges from multiple angles. Deloitte's 2020 Global Human Capital Trends[29] report reinforces this, highlighting that diverse teams excel at solving complex problems. In our industry, security challenges are multifaceted, and addressing them requires a range of viewpoints. Women bring critical insights into issues that affect not just the general population, but those of us who may face unique threats—issues like security risks targeting women, children, or marginalized communities. If we're not represented, these problems might not be addressed, and the solutions will fall short.

- Brittany Galli

---

[29] Vivian Hunt, Sara Prince, Sundiatu Dixon-Fyle, and Lareina Yee, *Diversity Wins: How Inclusion Matters* (McKinsey & Company, May 19, 2020), https://www.mckinsey.com/featured-insights/diversity-and-inclusion/diversity-wins-how-inclusion-matters

[29] Deloitte, *Global Human Capital Trends 2020: Superteams: Putting AI in the Group* (Deloitte Insights, 2020), https://www2.deloitte.com/us/en/insights/focus/human-capital-trends/2020.html

We asked: How has the industry evolved?

"The industry has not just changed its dress code; it has also transformed its purpose. When I started, corporate security had a reputation for being the 'corporate cop'. It is now a function that is more business-focused and proactive. In 2006, I co-wrote *The Business of Resilience*[30], which chronicled this transition, and I continue to hear from security professionals who have used the report for everything from researching their Master's thesis to writing their corporate security function's strategic review. **The move from reactive to proactive is probably the most significant trend I have witnessed.**

The community is also more varied than it was thirty years ago. At the beginning of my career, in most rooms I entered I was the only person who hadn't served in the military or law enforcement, the only woman, and the only person under the age of forty. There were almost no people of color, and we didn't talk about neurodiversity or sexual orientation. We can agree or disagree about whether things have gone too far or not far enough, but things have certainly changed. Corporate security teams now better reflect the workforce of the company they serve, and benefit from a wealth of complementary professional experiences. In a world where the problems we face are complicated, complex, and fast-moving, a multidimensional team is better placed than a homogeneous one to offer nuanced analysis and effective solutions."

– Rachel Briggs

"As private sector security evolved from traditional protective services to holistic security risk programs, it required more than just technical skills. Rapidly expanding and increasingly complex corporate security remits require leaders to be able to think and connect horizontally across organizations to build programs that are anticipatory, proactive, and more people-risk centric. From my experience, women in security have played a vital role in meeting this

---

[30] Rachel Briggs and Charlie Edwards, *The Business of Resilience: Corporate Security for the 21st Century* (London: Demos, 2006).

need because our natural caretaker instincts help us thrive in more ambiguous areas, require empathy, and need the ability to see the interconnectedness and consequences of action and inaction. **Women are transforming traditional security approaches and security cultures by leaning in to a softer, more person-focused approach that highlights the duty of care**. This combined hard and soft approach to security makes what we do more understandable for employees and leadership, increasing the ever-elusive 'buy-in.'"

- Sarah Slenker

What's next?

"**The next big change will be driven by technology**. Many corporate security functions are still analogue, using paper-based systems and Excel documents. Through simple and inexpensive investments, they can automate a range of processes to bring consistency and efficiency gains, and free up staff time for higher-value work.

The more technologically mature corporate security functions are experimenting with data lakes that join corporate security information with that from key parts of the business, such as the supply chain, to generate business-critical insights. They are enabling cyber and physical security technology to communicate in real time to cross-check access with system log-in information to spot unusual travel and potential insider behaviour. Some are asking how the data they hold as a function – security cameras, access control, for example – could help colleagues elsewhere in the business to solve their problems. Generative AI will, of course, supercharge all these efforts.

We have talked a lot in recent years about the importance of security professionals bringing their whole selves to work. **It is important that no one feels they must hide who they are or feel ashamed of their gender, sexual orientation, neurodiversity or alternative career background**. It's when we feel comfortable and confident that we do our best work.

Our unique qualities are also our teams' superpowers when we offer them in service of the problems we face together: experience being a lone female or LGBTQIA+ traveller incorporated into a travel security programme; previous work in a call centre applied to running a GSOC; time spent in another function bringing insight to help corporate security collaborate better; the tech-native Gen Z team member who assists innovation; or someone like me, who has first-hand experience of kidnapping, helping colleagues to better deal with the human fallout from crises and critical incidents."

- Rachel Briggs

"Security programs are stronger when you dig deeper into the 'causes' instead of the 'symptoms'. For a security program to be strong, it requires everyone's focus and understanding. I probably say this 50 times a day, "security is everyone's responsibility." As a woman it is easier for me to accept 'joint ownership.' I'm not threatened when other people do the right thing and help secure our company or our products. In fact, I want to highlight it. Seeking buy-in or partnerships is vital to everyone understanding the threats and risks, and moving forward in the best way possible for the company through mitigation. It's always been easier for me to collaborate. I don't think this is based on gender. I think it is based on mind-set."

- Wendy Bashnan

"**We bring a perspective that enriches and strengthens the overall effectiveness of any Corporate Security Program**. Security is not a one-size-fits-all endeavor. It requires diverse approaches, nuanced understanding, and a deep sense of empathy, qualities that our perspective helps to inform.

Our experiences give us the unique ability to recognize vulnerabilities that might go unnoticed in traditionally male-dominated spaces. Women often encounter security challenges differently, whether in public spaces, workplaces, or residential areas. This lived experience allows us to anticipate potential threats from angles others might not consider and to advocate for solutions that prioritize inclusivity and comprehensive safety measures.

Further, **our perspective challenges outdated stereotypes within the industry and inspires a broader culture of inclusivity.** I remember a time being the only female in a room of 100+ male security professionals. We have made some progress, but there is still a long way to go. **Promoting more women in security requires intentional efforts to address barriers, create opportunities, and build supportive environments.** Networking communities like Women in Security are essential for career professionals. Still, we must begin to nurture young girls and teens through outreach programs and community events during their formative years. Sharing stories of successful women in security can inspire girls, teens, and young women preparing for their next chapter to explore a career in Security, something they may never have considered prior. Further, our colleges and universities must offer scholarships, grants, and training programs specifically aimed at women pursuing security careers, and companies should explore creating pathways for women who are in school or with training to enter their workforce through security-specific internships, apprenticeships, and sector-specific professional security certifications.

When women are visible and active in Corporate Security leadership, it sends a powerful message about the importance of diversity in roles traditionally dominated by men. This diversity does not just enhance decision-making; it builds a strong, more representative, and resilient team. **Diverse leadership leads to stronger organizations**. Women leaders contribute to this success by prioritizing adaptability, emotional intelligence, and collaboration – traits essential for navigating the complexities of modern security challenges."

– *Mary Gates*

* * *

As the security industry evolves, it is the *vocal lanterns*, those leaders who speak up, share knowledge, and light the way, that will guide the next generation. Their insights and courage illuminate paths for innovation, inclusivity, and resilience, ensuring that the future of security is shaped not just by technology, but by people committed to making a meaningful difference. By listening to, learning from, and following these guiding lights, we can collectively build an industry that is brighter, stronger, and more adaptable than ever before.

9

Conclusion

Carrying the Light Forward

The stories shared in these pages reflect more than individual journeys; they reflect the evolving face of the security industry itself. An industry that is still growing, still shifting, and still learning what it means to be truly inclusive. These stories show the grit, the setbacks, the breakthroughs, and the quiet moments of doubt that so many of us know and most importantly, they remind us that none of us walk this path alone.

The reality is, there's still work to do. But we've seen what happens when women find their voice, build their networks, advocate for each other, and challenge the status quo. We've seen what's possible when allies step up, when boundaries are respected, when self-care isn't an afterthought, and when entrepreneurship, leadership, and bold ideas come from every corner of the world.

You don't have to have it all figured out to be part of shaping what comes next. You just have to be willing to keep learning, connecting, and lifting others along the way. Here's how you can stay connected and keep growing:

- **Find community**. Join professional groups, women in security networks, and mentorship circles. The more connected we are, the stronger we all become.
- **Keep learning**. Seek out training, certifications, and resources that build your confidence and expand your skills. Your growth doesn't stop here.
- **Be visible**. Share your story, your achievements, your lessons. it's not about ego, it's about paving the way for others.
- **Lift as you climb**. Advocate for women coming up behind you. Sponsor them. Make room at the table. The future depends on it.
- **Support initiatives that invest in the next generation**. Organizations like Girl Security are doing critical work to make sure tomorrow's leaders see security as a place where they belong.

The path isn't always clear. But as these stories have shown, we find our way and we light the way...together. Let's keep building what's next. Will you join us in becoming a *vocal lantern*?

Recommended Resources for Continued Growth & Connection

Girl Security - https://www.girlsecurity.org - Preparing girls, women, and gender minorities for careers in national and global security through education, mentorship, and workforce development.

ASIS International - Women in Security Community - https://www.asisonline.org/community/women-in-security - A professional network providing support, education, and advocacy for women across the security industry.

Security Industry Association (SIA) - Women in Security Forum -https://www.securityindustry.org/about-sia/committees/women-in-security-forum - Advancing leadership and opportunities for women in the security industry.

#ShareTheMicInCyber - https://www.sharethemicincyber.com - An initiative amplifying the voices of Black women in cybersecurity and promoting more equitable representation across the field.

Women in CyberSecurity (WiCyS) -https://www.wicys.org - A global community supporting the recruitment, retention, and advancement of women in cybersecurity through conferences, mentorship, and education.

Acknowledgments

The *Vocal Lanterns* project has been a true labor of love through which we have not only united the voices of incredibly powerful women and allies but also cultivated a community, reunited with friends, and felt tremendous support and love. We are humbled and grateful to acknowledge those who made this possible.

To our contributors: Thank you for sharing your wisdom and experiences, and for allowing us to gift them to others. This collection exists because of you, and we hope we have done you proud.

To Nick Young, Scott Jones, Kristin Lenardson, Nanette Levin, Holly Ford, and Mary Gates: Thank you for being so incredibly generous with your time, your talents, and your belief in us. Again and again, you have relit our lanterns throughout this journey.

To Lauren Bean Buitta and Girl Security: Thank you for the vital work you do to provide a path for the next generation of women in security. You show the world why we belong here, why we are needed here, and you give young women the tools, confidence, and strength to find their place in this industry. We are grateful for the opportunity to shine a light on your organization and contribute to its mission.

To those who personally contributed to the launch of this project: This endeavor has always been a work of the heart, and your generosity affirms both its meaning and its mission. With deep appreciation, we recognize Amanda Pritters, Liz Maloney, Melody Wen, Michelle La Plante, Olga Kocharyan, Paige

Wanless, Sweta Patel, and Suzanna Morrow for your financial support.

To our families and dear friends: Thank you for the grace you've given us as we navigated this process. Your unconditional love and support have carried us not only through this project but through life. We love you.

And finally, to our readers: Thank you. Know that you are lanterns for us, too.

Contributor Bios

Avila, Avila (*Chapters 1, 2, 3*)

Arian Avila is a Global Security and Technology leader for a Fortune 500 fintech organization. She's on a mission to learn, inspire, lift others and keep people safe in creative and innovative ways.

Mantra: The grass is greener where you water it.
Favorite quote: "Be water, my friend." - Bruce Lee

Bailey, Wendy (*Chapters 1, 2*)

Wendy Bailey has a thirty-plus-year security career in both the public and private sectors. She currently leads the Threat Management Team and the Care Team for Capital One. Wendy has a Bachelor's degree in Criminal Justice and is a Certified Threat Manager through the Association of Threat Assessment Professionals.

Theme song: "Unstoppable" by Sia

Bashnan, Wendy (*Chapters 1, 8*)

With an accomplished career in corporate security and law enforcement, Wendy Bashnan has worked across the globe. Specializing in corporate risk and resiliency, she advanced her career driving change that ensures organizations can evolve and grow. She's a confident and engaging communicator, who connects with multilevel/multicultural stakeholders to influence policy and decision-makers. Wendy builds consensus and changes mindsets, turning companies from reactive to proactive regarding risk and security. She was recognized as one of the '2022 Most Influential Security Professionals' by Security Magazine. She champions resiliency, implementing effective business continuity and crisis readiness plans that protect services and ensure rapid response.

Theme song: "Shake It" by The West Coast Feed
Mantra: "If I fear it, I will chase it." - Tyler Durden

Briggs, Rachel (*Chapters 1, 8*)

Rachel Briggs OBE is Founder and CEO of The Clarity Factory. She is a leading expert on corporate security and cyber security. She conducts research on latest trends and consults with clients to drive innovation and change within their teams. She is an Associate Fellow at Chatham House and was Founding Executive Director of Hostage US.

Theme song: "Dignity" by Deacon Blue

Campbell, Claire (*Chapters 1, 5*)

Claire Campbell has over twenty-five-years experience in public and private sector security programs and intelligence production. She is the founder of the LATAM Analysts Roundtable, an emeritus member of the OSAC Women in Security and LATAM Common Interest Councils, and current member of the OSAC MENA Common Interest Council. Claire speaks Spanish and Portuguese and is a graduate of St. Olaf College in Northfield, MN, and the University of Texas at Austin. She is also a contracted career coach and consultant with several major universities and non-profit institutions. Tacos are her love language.

Mantra: Adapt and overcome!

Carrington, Elena (*Chapter 3*)

Elena Carrington has two decades of experience in the security field, including tenures in an international organization, the aviation, technology, sports, and financial services industries, and the U.S. Department of State's Overseas Security Advisory Council. She currently leads the travel security, emergency response, and safety functions for a major accounting firm.

Mantra: "I've been here before." Meaning - if I'm struggling with something, I've faced challenges before and have overcome them.

De Leon, Gladis (*Chapters 2, 3, 6*)

Gladis De Leon is a Security and Risk leader who has led teams at Standard Industries, Swiss Re, Reckitt, and BASF. She entered the security world in 2015, having developed extensive experience in other corporate governance functions, including legal and internal audit. Gladis is passionate about diversity and inclusion, serving as both an informal and formal mentor through organizations such as ASIS and Girl Security.

Gladis holds a Master of Arts in Strategic Communication and Leadership, is a Certified Fraud Examiner, and a Certified Protection Professional.

Mantra: Don't ask questions you don't want answers to.

Deren, Eva *(Chapters 1, 3, 6)*

Eva Deren is the founder of Global Risk Overlay, LLC. She started her career at the UNICEF headquarters in New York City, gaining exposure to the issues facing vulnerable populations in Eastern Europe and the Commonwealth of Independent States. After obtaining a Master's degree in International Cooperation and Development from the Universidad Complutense de Madrid, she embarked upon a career in corporate intelligence analysis in oil & gas and the pharmaceutical industry which led her eventually to focus on crisis management.

Favorite quote: "Talk less. Smile more." - Lin Manuel-Miranda
Mantra: Live better, live longer.

Dominguez, Maria *(Chapters 1, 2)*

Maria Dominguez is an SVP/Ops and Program's manager and has been with Bank of America since May of 1999. Prior to that she worked for United Bank of Arizona, Citibank, Norwest Banks and Wells Fargo, without changing offices. Her career includes thirty-six years in the Security field, starting out as a security guard, after a one term of enlistment in the US Air Force.

Maria has BS in E-Business from the University of Phoenix and a Master's in Business and Organizational Security Management from Webster University, where she worked two year as an Associate Adjunct Professor at the Luke AFB campus of Webster University.

Favorite quote: "Do or do not, there is no try." - Yoda

Galli, Brittany (Chapters 5, 8)

Brittany Galli is a dedicated global security leader with expertise in designing and implementing elegant leadership strategies for innovation and organizational growth. She's known for her focus on technology and data-driven approaches and strives to help diversity thought at the C-suite level to make exponential change globally. Time to change the world!

Mantra: Remember, no matter where we are, who we work for or what we do each day:
  Speak your truth.
  Be Brave.
  Be bold and beautiful.
  Embrace your flaws, celebrate your wins.
  Hold your ground, spread love and take no shit.
  Don't play the victim, become the warrior.
  Know your worth, protect your energy and tell your story.
  Share your magic, laugh loud and proud and don't sweat the small stuff.
  Blow your own damn mind.

Gates, Mary (Chapters 1, 8)

Mary Gates is the President and Majority Owner of GMR Security, a physical security consulting, design, and managed services firm. Prior to leading GMR Security, Mary was the first Female Executive Director of Global Security and Investigations at JPMorgan Chase, where she led East Coast Physical Security Operations, Chase-branded Retail Security, and a host of other Security Programs over her twenty-five-year career with the Company. She is a long-tenured member of ASIS, where she is involved in several communities, and currently serves on the Banking and Financial Services Committee. Mary is also a member of the International Association of Professional Security

Consultants.

Favorite quote: 1 Peter 4:10 "As each has received a gift, use it to serve one another, as good stewards of God's varied grace." - The Holy Bible, English Standard Version

Hackman, Mary *(Chapters 1, 2)*

Mary Hackman has run intelligence and analytical programs for the US government and private sector for 23 years. She began at OSAC, at the State Department's Diplomatic Security Bureau, and also held positions at Navanti, managing analytical programs supporting the US military and USAID, and DHS's Office of Intelligence & Analysis. She then moved to Visa's Global Security team, where she is responsible for global intelligence, workforce protection, and the GSOC.

Ms. Hackman has a Master's degree in Conflict Analysis from George Mason University, and a BA from Indiana University. She lives with her husband and two sons in Virginia.

Favorite book: *Tribe* by Sebastian Junger

Harbour, Tiffany *(Chapter 2)*

Dr. Tiffany Harbour is a public policy professional with over twenty years' experience in the international community, in both public and private sectors. She has led several efforts across industry sectors in working with government authorities, trade associations, non-governmental organizations, and civic groups to address security, policy, and resilience.

Tiffany now calls Charlotte, North Carolina, home, having moved here to serve as Bank of America's Senior Vice President for International Public Policy, covering Latin America and Asia Pacific. These are two regions which her current security work is focused for an international non-governmental organization focused on disaster response and preparedness. Tiffany is a US Army veteran.

Favorite quote: "In the middle of every difficulty lies opportunity." - Albert Einstein

Hern, Jessica *(Chapters 1, 2)*

Jessica Hern is the Director for Risk & Resilience in Global Security at 3M, where she manages global risk and threat assessment and mitigation, global intelligence analysis, the Global Security Operations Center (GSOC), crisis management, and business resilience programs. Prior to joining 3M, Ms. Hern directed the Global Intelligence function at St. Jude Medical, where she oversaw global security risk assessment, investigations, incident and crisis management, and threat mitigation. Ms. Hern also worked in the U.S. Government intelligence community on analysis of foreign leadership and information operations and in the U.S. Department of Justice's international rule-of-law development office. Ms. Hern holds a Bachelor of Arts from St. Olaf College in Northfield, MN and a Master of International Affairs from Columbia University's School of International and Public Affairs in New York, NY. She also holds a graduate certificate in Enterprise Risk Management from Carnegie Mellon University.

Favorite quote: "She had always wanted words, she loved them; grew up on them. Words gave her clarity, brought reason, shape." - from *The English Patient*, by Michael Ondaatje[23]

Jones, Scott *(Chapter 4)*

Jonesy enjoys focusing on next generation innovation, value-based change management, and organizational transformation for leaders and groups evolving to exceed customer expectations. They have direct experience in addressing operational effectiveness, identifying long-term success measures, forecasting, crisis management, strategic planning, contracts and procurement, and reputation risk. Jonesy is also passionate about employee development, DEI, and visioning through coaching and mentoring.

Mantra: Everyone deserves to thrive in safe, healthy, and vibrant communities

Kennedy-Boudali, Lianne *(Chapter 3)*

Lianne Kennedy-Boudali's career has spanned multiple organizations and industries. She is currently the leader of a multi-disciplinary risk consulting practice within Control Risks; she previously served as chief strategy officer and intelligence lead at a security consulting firm; as the managing director of an international research group based in Abu Dhabi; as a policy analyst in the National Security Research Division of RAND Corporation; as an instructor in the Social Sciences department of the United States Military Academy at West Point and a researcher in the Combating Terrorism Center; and as a US Peace Corps Volunteer in Niger. She holds a Master of International Affairs degree from Columbia University and a Bachelor of Arts degree from the University of California Santa Cruz. In all her roles, she focuses on solving complex problems through creativity and collaboration.

Favorite quote: "A ship is safe in harbor, but that is not what ships are built for." - John A. Shedd

Kocharyan, Olga *(Chapters 3, 6)*

Olga Kocharyan is an Insider Threat Manager with thirteen years of experience across global corporate security and cybersecurity for financial institutions. Her experience includes physical identity access management, insider investigations, breach and attack simulation, and strategic business enablement and operations. As a champion in STEM programs and affinity groups, as well as a mentor for FS-ISAC and Grace Hopper scholarship recipients at Bank of America, she was presented several prestigious awards including the Diversity & Inclusion Award and Delivering One Company Award. She holds four granted patents with an additional dozen published in areas including multidimensional disparate user data, NFTs, and secure tokenization.

Favorite quotes: "Life is not about waiting for the storm to pass, it's about learning to dance in the rain." - Vivian Green

"This too shall pass." - Abraham Lincoln

Komendat, Dave *(Chapter 4)*

Dave Komendat is the President of DSKomendat Risk Management Services, a security risk management consultancy. Prior to this role, he was the Vice President & Chief Security Officer for The Boeing Company, a position he held for fourteen of my thirty-six year Boeing career. He currently serves on the Board of Directors for The Security Foundation and Hostage US.

Favorite quote: "Security is always too much until the day it is not enough" Judge William Webster, retired Director, FBI and CIA

La Plante, Michelle *(Chapter 1)*

Michelle La Plante leads TE Connectivity's geopolitical risk and business resiliency strategies. Prior to joining TE, Michelle established and led John Deere's strategic intelligence unit after having served on Deere's international government affairs team, where she advocated for competitive trade and investment environments in overseas markets, focusing on high-tech supply chain resiliency.

Michelle previously served as an economic analyst with the U.S. Department of State at the Embassies in Moscow and Beijing where she worked on bilateral trade and security issues. In Beijing, Michelle was twice awarded a Meritorious Honor Award from Ambassador Baucus for her coverage of the Asian Infrastructure Investment Bank and the Bilateral Investment Treaty. Before her tenure at the State Department, Michelle worked as a project finance lawyer in California, London, and New York, where her practice specialized in automated toll roads. Michelle is fluent in Spanish and earned a B.A. in Communication Studies from UCLA, and a Juris Doctor from UC Law San Francisco. She lives in Arlington, Virginia with her husband and three children.

Favorite song: "Mama Said Knock You Out" by LL Cool J

Lavinder, Kathy (*Chapters 2, 7*)

Kathy Lavinder has twenty-five years' experience in executive search, working with multinational corporations, financial institutions, professional services firms, academic and healthcare institutions, family offices, and non-profits to identify specialized talent for security, investigations, and intelligence functions.

Lavinder founded Security & Investigative Placement Consultants in 2000 after working in investigative roles and broadcast journalism. As an investigator, Lavinder was with a prominent investigations boutique in Washington, DC. She served as the head of the firm's headquarters. Early in her career, Lavinder was with ABC News in New York.

Lavinder's undergraduate degree is from the University of South Carolina, and she has a Master's degree from Georgetown University.

Favorite quote: "It's not the honors and not the titles and not the power that is of ultimate importance. It's what resides inside." - Fred Rogers

Lenardson, Kristin *(Chapters 1, 6)*

Twenty-plus-year security professional in the public and private sectors. Director of Security at The Scion Group, and a Chicago-native. Mom, mentor, aspiring comedian, and Peloton owner (but not an obnoxious one.)

Favorite quote: "Aut viam inveniam aut faciam. (I shall either find a way or make one.)" - General Hannibal Barca

Lewis, Angela *(Chapter 3)*

Dr. Angela Miller Lewis is the Head of Global Intelligence, Investigations, and Threat Management at Creative Artists Agency (CAA). She also serves as an Adjunct Professor, teaching courses in counterterrorism, intelligence, and advanced analytic techniques at Georgetown University, the University of New Hampshire, and the University of Cincinnati. Dr. Lewis earned her Ph.D. in Global Leadership from Pepperdine University, focusing on intelligence for strategic decision-making. She previously served as a senior targeting officer in the CIA's Directorate of Operations with multiple tours abroad and has held security leadership roles at Salesforce and Disney.

Favorite quote: "Embrace uncertainty. Some of the most beautiful chapters in our lives won't have a title until much later." - Bob Goff

Lincke, Janina *(Chapters 2, 3)*

Janina Lincke is a skilled security professional, experienced in corporate GSOCs, Business Threat Intelligence, Protective Intelligence, Close Protection, and Emergency Medical Response.

Janina holds a BSC Honors degree from the University of Stellenbosch, has completed both Ronin courses in Close Protection and Emergency Medical Response. She is an Intermediate Life Support Medic, and has worked for ambulance services in Mexico, South Africa and the UK. Janina's global EP contracts include serving Royals, Executives, UHNI, and Politicians.

She currently leads a team of intelligence analysts in a global security company, combining Operational and Business Threat Intelligence capabilities in an elite facility. She has previously headed an ASIS working group establishing global Executive Protection standards.

Favorite quote: "You can do hard things." - Glennon Doyle

Maloney, Liz *(Chapters 1, 6)*

Liz Maloney is a Solutions Architect in Cyber Defense Operations at Microsoft. She was a program manager for Microsoft's cyber threat intelligence team and led Microsoft's Global Security intelligence program for over ten years, building it from the ground up to became one of the premiere Intelligence organizations in the corporate space globally. Liz is dedicated to fostering cohesive teams and cultivating analysts.

Favorite passage: "Man in the Arena" - Theodore Roosevelt

Martinez, Jessica *(Chapters 1, 2, 5, 6, 7)*

Jessica Martinez is an organizational culture and effectiveness leader and the founder of Tomorrow's Office, a performance consulting firm focused on redefining how we work for the next generation. She has over a decade of experience driving operational change, communications, and employee experience at Fortune 500 companies, including strategic leadership roles through two of the largest mergers and acquisitions in tech and entertainment history. She most recently served as the first Head of Culture at Blizzard Entertainment, where she led the company through a redefinition of its mission and legacy values following allegations of a toxic workplace. Jessica frequently writes and speaks on culture, leadership, and the intersection of career and parenthood.

Mantra: "Why not?" as a response to "We can't do that."

Favorite quote: "Every zoo is a petting zoo if you're brave enough." - Anonymous

Morrow, Suzanna *(Chapters 1, 2, 6)*

Suzanna Morrow served as the Senior Director of Global Security Intelligence and Due Diligence for Meta Platforms, leading a global department focused on supporting Meta operations. Prior to her tenure at Meta, Suzanna served in multiple capacities at the Defense Intelligence Agency and within the U.S. Defense Department. She has a Bachelor's degree in Economics and Asian Studies from Northwestern University and a Master's degree in Strategic Intelligence from the National Intelligence University. She served on the Client Advisory Board for Emergent Risk International and as the President of the Board of the Association of International Risk Intelligence Professionals. She currently teaches as an adjunct instructor at Mercyhurst University's Department of Intelligence Studies.

Favorite quote: "I wasn't lucky, I deserved it." - Margaret Thatcher

Muir, Melissa *(Chapter 1)*

Melissa Muir bridges the worlds of human resources and threat assessment, bringing over twenty-five years of experience building safety through innovative people practices. After HR leadership roles in the public sector, she now consults with organizations to implement effective prevention strategies.

As a leader with the Association of Threat Assessment Professionals (ATAP), Melissa trains globally on building effective partnerships between security and HR, with engaging presentations from "How Not to Hire a Psychopath" to "How to Say Goodbye." She holds an MBA from the University of Washington and a JD from Seattle University School of Law.

Favorite quote: "There comes a point where we need to stop just pulling people out of the river. We need to go upstream and find out why they're falling in." - Desmond Tutu

Nayyar, Alyssa *(Chapters 1, 3, 6)*

Alyssa Nayyar started her career in the private security industry in 2015 after leaving the education sector. She held significant roles at Target Corporation, Capital One Financial, and Netflix, where she gained extensive experience in building and managing travel security programs, managing global crisis events as a GSOC manager, and leading intelligence programs with a focus on Latin America and the US. She is particularly known in the industry for her expertise in driving continuous improvements in the travel security space. Alyssa is currently the Chief Operating Officer at Sibylline, where she is dedicated to creating a culture where all employees can thrive.

Favorite quote: "Wake Up, Kick Ass, Be Kind, Repeat" - Sharon Grigsby

O'Neill, Peggy *(Chapter 2)*

Peggy F. O'Neill was appointed Executive Director of the nonprofit The Security Foundation (TSF) in 2013. TSF's mission is to enable impactful collaboration throughout the security industry. A nonprofit leader specializing in startups, turnarounds, and leadership coaching, Peggy has over forty years of experience working with boards and creating successful and innovative financial models to grow organizations. Past positions included CFO at the Whitby School in Greenwich, Connecticut, and a six-year tenure as executive director of the Irvine Nature Center, an environmental education organization near Baltimore, Maryland.

Favorite quote: "I refuse to believe that you cannot be both compassionate and strong." - Jacinda Ardern, PM New Zealand

Parkes, Haylea *(Chapters 2, 3)*

Haylea Parkes leads Security & Resilience at CBRE, ensuring the resilience of company people, clients, partners, and business. Haylea develops and delivers physical security, business continuity, and crisis management strategies across CBRE's operations and is a trusted advisor to CBRE's global leaders to address risks and promote a resilient organizational culture. Haylea has over two decades of experience in risk, compliance and business resilience across diverse industries, including commercial real estate, utility services, banking and finance.

Favorite quote: "Don't let perfect be the enemy of good." - Gretchen Rubin

Patel, Sweta *(Chapters 3, 6)*

Since joining Lowe's in 2020 as a senior manager of GSOC and Intelligence, Sweta Patel has been a pivotal change agent while providing strategic direction to the Global Security Operations Center (GSOC) and Business Continuity teams. Sweta, with her team, built the company's first GSOC and enterprise threat intelligence function, aimed at proactively identifying various threats, trends, and events and providing timely crisis communications to key stakeholders. She is also responsible for enhancing business continuity and crisis support procedures: the team who works diligently across the enterprise to identify critical processes and help business units develop contingency plans to ensure the continuation of services throughout various disruptions.

Sweta has more than thirteen years of experience in strategic and tactical intelligence as well as GSOCs and has recently taken responsibility for Business Continuity programs. She began her career at Bank of America as Intelligence /Research Specialist, became shift manager of GSOC Operations and analyst with Enterprise Event Response functions before moving to Wells Fargo as Business Initiatives Consultant as part of the Corporate Security Intelligence program.

Sweta earned a bachelor's degree in accounting and finance from The Maharaja Sayajirao University of Baroda, India and possesses Executive Leadership certification from Cornell University. Sweta holds a Crisis Management for leaders' certification from Stanford University of Graduate School of Business. She also brings professional bona fides with her certification in Business Continuity.

Favorite quote: "You are the biggest ambassador of your personal brand! Own Your Story and Excel at it!!" - Jeff Bezos

Patra, Andreea *(Chapters 1, 6)*

Andreea Patra graduated from Mercyhurst College with a degree in Intelligence Studies and Spanish. She joined Bank of America in 2008 as a Due Diligence Investigator and shortly after had the opportunity to join Corporate Security as an intelligence analyst, focused on the Western US, Latin America, and Canada. She was fortunate to have amazing leaders, mentors, and sponsors who guided (and often gave her a little-needed nudge) in the right direction. She grew to lead various teams under the Corporate Security umbrella, including the COVID Intelligence team. She is now the Intelligence and Analysis Director for Global Corporate Security and Executive Protection.

Mantra: Don't just aspire to make a living - aspire to make a difference! Take chances and fail big!

Phair, Jaime *(Chapter 3)*

Proud mom of two girls, wife, stepmom, and twenty-plus years as a Global Security Leader within a Fortune 100 Transportation company.

Favorite quote: "Be a Goldfish." - Ted Lasso

Provence, Kirsten *(Chapters 1, 5)*

As the Executive Director of Kaiser Permanente's National Security Services, Kirsten Provence leads the team responsible for security programs, including Prevention of Workplace Violence and Threat Management, Security Communications, Corporate Security Investigations, and Security Training. She is also responsible for the governance and quality improvement of security services.

Kirsten has a degree in Political Science and an MBA in Business Administration, Global Management. Kirsten joined Kaiser Permanente in 2022 after a more than twenty-year career in the aerospace and defense industry. In addition to her organizational duties, she has served on many industry committees and boards and has been honored for her leadership skills by multiple publications.

Mantra: What gets measured, gets done.

Rice, Liz *(Chapters 1, 7)*

Liz Rice is a seasoned security operations leader and business consultant with deep expertise in building high-performing teams and enterprise-shared services. She has led and developed over 3,000 healthcare security professionals nationwide and held senior roles, including Senior Vice President of Security Operations and Vice President of Security Strategy. Liz has supported Fortune 500 organizations like Kaiser Permanente and PG&E in designing scalable, people-centered security models. Recognized as a SIA Power 100 Woman, she is also a mentor, strategist, and founder of Z Multiplier LLC—driven by a mission to uplift talent and create safer, stronger organizations through leadership, coaching, and operational excellence.

Favorite quote: "Comparison is the thief of joy" - Theodore Roosevelt

Mantra: Fail Forward

Favorite book: *Unapologetically Ambitious* by Shellye Archambeau

Rowe, Michelle *(Chapter 3)*

Michelle Rowe is a security professional with over nineteen years of experience, currently serving as the APAC Regional Security Director for Physical Security Operations at Meta. She spent her first twenty-five years in the fitness industry, which included work within the film industry as an individual contractor and as a small business owner/operator of a training facility.

Favorite quote: "The best way to get started is to quit talking and begin doing." - Walt Disney

Sands, Allison *(Chapter 3)*

Allison Sands is the VP of Security at Gilead Sciences. She previously served in security roles at NBC Universal and Roku, and in the U.S. government as a Presidential Management Fellow for the U.S. Navy, an intelligence analyst for the Department of Defense, and a Special Agent with the FBI. She is a Director of the Silicon Valley Security Group, a mentor for Girl Security, and the President of the Board of Directors at W.O.M.A.N. Inc. She lives in Walnut Creek, California with her husband and ten pound "security" dog.

Mantra: Turn "why me" into "try me"

Sanya, Julia *(Chapters 1, 6)*

Julia Sanya is the Sr. Manager of Regional Security and leads physical security operations at Capital One's growing HQs and mixed-use campus, Capital One Center, in Tysons, Virginia. Julia has responsibility for leading strategic planning and execution of Capital One's security operations programs and services. Julia is a business enabler with expertise in designing strategic scalable security solutions and services that meet the needs of the business and pushes the boundaries of what can be accomplished.

Julia has over sixteen years of experience in both corporate and retail security, investigations and loss prevention for Fortune 500 companies. She holds a BA in Criminology and Criminal Justice from University of Maryland, CPP and CFE certifications, and was recognized as Security Magazine's "Security's 2022 Women in Security." Julia is a DEI and social impact advocate with previous experience in leading department DEI and Pro Bono programs, as well as serving on internal business resource group steering committees.

Favorite quotes: "Who you are is who you are. If you can't be who you are where you are, change where you are, not who you are." - Caroline Wanga
"The most meaningful way to succeed is to help others succeed." - Adam Grant

Slenker, Sarah *(Chapter 8)*

Sarah A. Slenker, CPP, is a seasoned global security executive with over twenty-five years of experience in the security industry. Beginning her career as a competitive intelligence and global security analyst, Sarah's latest role was the Head of Safety and Security at a Fortune 2000 company. Sarah's expertise encompasses a broad spectrum of domains, including security program strategy, travel risk management, geopolitical intelligence analysis, security risk management, policy development, and program implementation. She has built and led dynamic, global teams of safety and security professionals entrusted with safeguarding the well-being of employees, clients, and assets worldwide.

Favorite quote: "When one door closes another door opens; but we so often look so long and so regretfully upon the closed door, that we do not see the ones which open for us." - Attributed to Alexander Graham Bell

Stephens, Brian *(Chapter 4)*

Senior Managing Director, Teneo Security Risk Advisory, former global Chief Security Officer at Bank of America

Favorite song: "Tin Cup for a Chalice" by Jimmy Buffet

Favorite quote: "The time is always right to do what's right" - Martin Luther King Jr.

Stone, Maria *(Chapter 2)*

Maria Stone is a Head of Global Intelligence with McDonald's, where she leads a team of geopolitical risk analysts and also manages the protective intelligence function. Prior to joining McDonald's, Maria was a Director of Crisis Management and Resilience with Kenvue (Johnson and Johnson family of companies), where she built the ERM and Crisis Management programs. Maria spent ten years with Abbott, where she led several risk intelligence and crisis management roles and teams, as well as a cybersecurity function. Maria also helped to build and shape a geo-political risk function at United Airlines and Archer Daniels Midland. Maria was born and raised in Russia, where she obtained her Law Degree before moving to the United States. Maria holds a Master of Arts degree from Illinois State University and MBA degree from the Lake Forest Graduate School of Management.

Favorite quote: "Never give up! No matter what!" - Winston Churchill

Surve, Pranoti *(Chapters 1, 2)*

Forged in Mumbai and moulded by the world, Pranoti's personal driver has been to find a stimulating ecosystem of people, places, and purpose. For over 15 years, she's built and led global security, risk, and crisis programs across finance, tech, and consumer sectors. From protecting people to climate resilience, safeguarding the value chain to cross-border data governance, and embedding human rights in security, Pranoti navigated complexity with clarity and anchored strategy in moments of ambiguity. Her work spans continents, but the goal is constant: build trust, reduce harm, and lead with intent. Resilience isn't toughness, it's adaptation. It's knowing when to listen, when to act, and how to walk the line between foresight and resolve.

Mantra: Prioritize long-term respect over short-term popularity.

Teng, Lillian *(Chapters 1, 2)*

Lillian Teng, a cybersecurity leader and mom (to a kiddo, a doggo, and many houseplants!), has a career spanning government, technology, consulting, and finance. A Georgetown University graduate, she began as a Cyber Special Agent with the Naval Criminal Investigative Service (NCIS) in 2003, serving in the Middle East and Asia. In 2011, she moved to Booz Allen Hamilton, supporting the FBI's Cyber Division. After over a decade of government service, Lillian shifted to the private sector, leading teams at Yahoo and Capital One.

Passionate about community, Lillian focuses on food insecurity, sustainability, and amplifying women and underrepresented groups in STEM, particularly cybersecurity. She serves on the advisory boards of the KC7 Foundation and GirlSecurity, and joined the board of Leadership Education for Asian Pacifics (LEAP) in 2022.

Favorite Quote: I drink and I know things. - Tyrion Lannister, *Game of Thrones*

Vaccaro, Tristin *(Chapter 7)*

Tristin Vaccaro is the owner of Vaccaro Copywriting & Marketing Solutions, a thriving freelance agency that serves the physical security industry. Here, she partners with various organizations to produce impactful content that connects with target audiences. Her collaborators know her as a highly creative individual who can always be trusted to come up with a new approach.

As a proud member of the SIA RISE Committee and chair of the DE&I Subcommittee, Tristin is passionate about advancing diversity, equity, and inclusion initiatives within the security sector.

Mantra: If you knew it would all work out, would you enjoy it more along the way?

Van Horn, Dorian *(Chapters 1, 3)*

Dorian Van Horn, MS, retired as a Special Agent, NCIS, Division Chief, TMU/InT as well as the Family & Sexual Violence unit and SSA for Violent Crime, Death, Cold Case Homicide, and Special Interest Investigations. She is the ATAP National 1st VP and was awarded the ATAP Meritorious Service Award. She is trained in Forensic Linguistics and the Stalking Risk Profile. She was appointed by the Secretary of Defense as a Government Advisor, DSB Task Force, Predicting Violent Behavior. She is an advisor to the DHS, Office of intelligence and Analysis, NTER Program, the DHS NCITE Center, as well as the Violence/Threat Assessment Advisory Work Group, National Suicide Prevention Lifeline. She was a member of the ATAP Certification and Development team for the CTM Examination and the revision of the RAGE-V. Her publications include: *The International Handbook of Threat Assessment*; *DSB Final Report, Predicting Violent Behavior*; and "School of Threats," *Security Management Magazine*.

Favorite quote: "Bloom where you are planted" - Saint Francis de Sales

Vitello, Corey *(Chapter 4)*

Corey Vitello is an experienced Safety & Security leader, strategist, program-builder, and risk manager. As Senior Director and Head of Global Security & Workplace Solutions at Roku, Corey leads strategy, planning, operations, intelligence and risk analyses, crisis management, the enterprise threat management team, program governance, compliance, and a whole host of additional leadership initiatives. Corey has been with Roku since April 2022.

Corey joined the leadership team as the Chief Security Officer for Prometheus

Fuels in August 2020. His responsibilities included personnel and facility security operations, threat monitoring and assessment, environmental health and safety, crisis management, information security and data privacy. Prior to this role, he held the position of Head of Global Security Operations for Stripe, where he and his team created international security programs, established governance and compliance processes, and provided duty of care in over a dozen countries for the company's fast-scaling workforce. Before Stripe, Corey was Senior Director of Global Security and Safety for Visa.

Academically, Corey holds a Doctor of Philosophy in Forensic Psychology and a Master of Arts in Organizational Behavior from Alliant International University.

Favorite quotes: "Fortune favors the bold" - Roman poet Virgil

"When in doubt, confer." - Benjamin Franklin

Walters, Jennifer *(Chapters 1, 2)*

Jennifer Walters is a security leader based in Charlotte, North Carolina. Her decades-long career leading corporate security teams—focused on strategy, innovation, and risk mitigation—has been fueled by her core values: protecting the people, operations, and assets of major financial institutions.

She is a vocal champion for advancing diversity in the security industry, working to challenge traditional norms and empower underrepresented professionals to thrive in security roles.

Favorite quote: "Just keep swimming" - Dory, *Finding Nemo*

Wanless, Paige *(Chapters 3, 6)*

Paige Wanless works for Bank of America's Global Corporate Security & Executive Protection. In this role, Paige manages the physical security exercise program where she facilitates exercises of facilities, teams, and work processes to measure readiness and response to physical security threats. In addition to the exercise program, Paige also manages the Kidnap for Ransom and Hostage Response programs and is the Corporate Security representative for Bank of America's Human Trafficking Taskforce. In her spare time, she enjoys spending time with her family, being outdoors, staying active, and baking.

Favorite quote: "You better walk into that room like God sent you there, because he did. This is not a time for doubts or insecurities, this is a time for confidence in who God says who you are, and the value you bring." - Benjamin Lundquist

Wen, Melody (Chapters 1, 5)

Melody Wen is a Resilience leader with experience spanning technology, finance, and aerospace industries. Her passion emerged from volunteering with the American Red Cross, aiding New Yorkers in crises. She's an advocate for resiliency programs to reflect the communities, customers, and clients that these programs serve. Melody is especially passionate about helping women break into the field, flourishing as leaders, and building bridges to help the next generation of resiliency professionals. She holds an MPA in Emergency Management and serves on DRII's Women in Business Continuity Management Executive Committee.

Favorite quote: "Look for the helpers. You will always find people who are helping." - Fred Rogers

Wilson, Meredith (Chapters 1, 7)

CEO and Founder, global traveler, writer, mom, partner, entrepreneur, hot yoga devotee, life-long learner, and a firm believer in the church of lifting all boats and "sending the elevator back down."

Favorite quote: "If it were easy, everyone would do it." - Phil Williams

About the Editors

Arian Avila

Arian Avila currently leads Workplace Services Technology and Security Operations for a major technology and financial institution. Her journey into corporate security began while pursuing her Ph.D. in Criminology at Northeastern University, when Bank of America offered her a position as their first crime analyst, charged with reducing bank robbery numbers. That opportunity launched her into a distinguished career in private sector safety and security.

Her leadership extends beyond corporate walls as a founding member of Global Security Pride, an organization dedicated to supporting and elevating the LGBTQIA+ community within the security field. She also supports private-public partnerships through leadership involvement in the FBI's Domestic Security Alliance Council (DSAC) and increasing engagement and advancement through her work with The Security Foundation (TSF). In 2024, she was named by Security Magazine as one of the Most Influential People in Security.

She earned her Bachelor's degree in Psychology and Master's degree in Criminal Justice from California State University, Long Beach, and is currently finishing her Doctorate at the University of North Carolina at Charlotte. When not immersed in security strategy or doctoral studies, she enjoys gaming with her kids, browsing independent bookstores, and indulging in musical theater and 80s pop culture.

Jennifer Walters

Jennifer Walters is a security leader based in Charlotte, NC. Her decades-long career leading corporate security teams—focused on strategy, innovation, and risk mitigation—has been fueled by her core values: protecting the people, operations, and assets of major financial institutions.

She is a vocal champion for advancing diversity in the security industry, working to challenge traditional norms and empower underrepresented professionals to thrive in security roles. Through her writing, speaking engagements, and mentorship, she inspires current and future security leaders to think differently and embrace diversity not only as a value—but as a strategic advantage.

Jennifer is a single mother of four, with a grandchild on the way. She is an avid reader, enjoys writing whimsical short stories about her life's adventures, and maintains a rotating catalogue of hobbies. She strives to live by the words "find joy," and enthusiastically encourages everyone in her life to do the same.